Auntie and the Girl

First published in 2016 by Reed Independent, Victoria, Australia.

Printed by Createspace.com, a division of Amazon.com.

Available as a printed book or an ebook from Createspace.com or Amazon.com or Kindle estores, together with most major international online outlets or bookshops with online ordering facilities:
paperback: ISBN 9780994531162
ebook: ISBN 9780994531179

Copyright © Bill Reed 2016

Front cover: Images from Google Images. Design by Dilani Priyangika Ranaweera, Dart Lanka Productions

National Library of Australia Cataloguing-in-Publication entry:
Creator: Reed, Bill, author.
Title: Auntie and the Girl/ Bill Reed
Edition: first
ISBN: 9780994531162 (paperback)
ISBN: 9780994531179 (ebook)
Notes: includes bibliographical reference.
Subjects: Drama/infanticide/black comedy
Dewey Number: A822.3

Auntie and the Girl

a play
Bill Reed

Also by Bill Reed

Plays
Burke's Company
Bullsh/ More Bullsh
Cass Butcher Bunting
Mr Siggie Morrison with his Comb and Paper
Truganinni
Living in Black Holes (anthology)
Living on Mars (anthology)
Living on Mars: the play
Daddy the 8th
Truganinni Inside Out
Auntie and the Girl
Mirror, Mirror
Little She
You Want It, Don't You, Billy?
The Pecking Order
Jack Charles is Up and Fighting
Just Out of Your Ground
I Don't Know What to Do with You!
Paddlesteamer

novels
The Pipwink Papers\
Me, the Old Man
Stigmata
Ihe
Dogod
Crooks
Tusk
Throw her back
Are You Human?
Tasker Tusker Tasker
Awash
1001 Lankan Nights book 1
1001 Lankan Nights book 2
Passing Strange

Nonfiction
Water Workout

Award-winning short stories (see also title 'Passing Strange')
Messman on the C.E. Altar
The 200-year Old Feet
The Case Inside
Blind Freddie Among the Pickle Jars
The Old Ex-serviceman
The Shades of You my Dandenong

AUNTIE AND THE GIRL was workshopped by the then Playbox Theatre in 2007 and was shortlisted for the Australasian-wide Australia-Asia Theatre Award in the same year. It has been on the verge of numerous seasons over recent years, but I guess either Auntie or the girl, or both, are true in life to their stage natures and remain contrarians to the idea.

It is also available as a chosen script by the Australian Script Centre through its website Australianplays.org.

The Characters

AUNTIE
Mrs Sathianathan, but maiden name Jones. She is Australian, now aged 76, living in India and has done so for the last 50 years since marrying Mr S., a plantation officer. Thin but as hard-edged as a garden rake. Her age has heightened her eccentric character but, of course, made it more socially acceptable. Her self-indulgence and venality is now only hilarious. Her snobbery -- maintained, even though Mr S. was never more than a Chief Clerk in tea plantations and she an unqualified English teacher -- her character is blustered by the dynamic praying she is into. Her favourite saying: 'Look out, Madam Mountain coming through!'.

SHANTI
The girl. Auntie's domestic. Fourteen years of age, she is from a poor low-caste Indian family. She has been sent to Chennai from the village to work as a domestic and got lumbered with Auntie. She will develop into a know-it-all and even now won't be left out of anything. Top flight in English; will always try to sneak into the top of the queue. Backward steps she doesn't know.

NAVIN
The doctor son of AUNTIE who has come back to India to live with her. He is a gynaecologist, an assistant District Medical Officer (= assistant coroner), but maintains his own birth control clinic. He is getting to middle-age but yet is a bachelor, even though, in Indian, he is top marriageable material. Wouldn't want to be blamed for 'it'… it meaning anything and everything. The character he presents?: 'I specialise in the field of foetus-gender determination and concomitant correctional services'.

DOROTHY
Auntie's daughter-in-law. An Australian living in Sydney and in her late thirties, she married DAVID, the eldest of Auntie's four children. He was a topmost brain surgeon in Australia, but killed

in Sydney under the worst of circumstances... so bad in fact that Dorothy has thought – against her better nature -- that it only right that she comes to Chennai to tell Auntie what really happened face-to-face. She is an impatient woman, rather than nervy; simmering rather than aggressive. She also prides herself on calling a spade a spade... but, when emotionally pushed, she shows herself to be surprisingly flustering, especially when it comes to social issues she considers of the moral kind.

CHARLES EKANAYAKE
A Chief Inspector of police from Sri Lanka. He is a longtime friend of the Sathianathan family; indeed, he owes much to Auntie from when she was virtually his second mother when he boarded with them in his school days. Now in Chennai, he is staying there again, while he completes his year's secondment to the Indian CBI regarding the Tamil (now criminal rather than terrorist) ethnic problems back in Sri Lanka. He is a proud, tall/gangly with hawkish features, honest cop... so weirdly different to his fellow Lankans in looks and outlook. Has a hunter's fierce unforgiving instinct. Still struggles with his English after all the years of using the language professionally, and is more than a bit of a sufferer of Tourette syndrome with his 'bloodypuckinghell... sorry, sorry!'s.

Act 1

(The central room of Auntie's house in Chennai. It is quite a large house and this large central space combines a sort of casual bedroom plus living and dining rooms. There are here cabinets and large book cases (filled with torn old secondhand paperbacks). Off from this room are no less than three bedrooms. Central to all is the TV. The opening to the kitchen to the right has no door.

A sharp eye might notice that the furnishings are dominated by duty-free items. These have come from her two daughters living in Canada and her son David living in Australia. That same sharp eye might notice very little in the way of family photographs or memorabilia.

The main background noise is from the nearby main road. In India this is considerable and can be used dramatically, as necessary.

It is early Sunday morning. Already the traffic is 'getting up'. We hear this increasing over the soft snores of NAVIN, who is sleeping on the large king-sized bed in the middle of the room.
Note: as is common in Indian households, people will use this bed as a communal seat, even visitors, to chat or to watch TV or both at the same time.

Soon we hear annoyance from one of the bedrooms.

EKANAYAKE hurries out of his room, dressing as he comes (civilian clothes), running very late for something.)

EKANAYAKE: (calling) Auntie, I am going for your Dorothy. Late, late, bloodypuckinghell, sorry sorry.

(He hurries out.

For a time, there is no movement.

Then the dark little form of SHANTI scampers out of AUNTIE's room on all fours, making for the TV She switches the TV on and settles back to watch (with boisterous mimicry) an IPL T20 cricket replay. NAVIN is not in the least disturbed sleeping there, although he has his head covered.

But she suddenly gets an attack of nausea. {She is terribly theatrical about it, hand over mouth, puff cheeks, prodding NAVIN and so forth.} When she can resist it no longer, she dashes for the front door, which has been unbolted by EKANAYAKE when he left, and...

... simply chucks up on the front doorstep in plain view, as though too earthly tired to move past the front door once she took the effort to open it.

NAVIN slides out of bed groaningly. He goes seedily over to her, pats her back until she finishes. Then he helps lift her and escorts her back to being in front of the TV again. This, she watches again, as though nothing has disrupted her viewing.

He goes to the sink by the dining room table, wets a much-used, therefore dirty, towel and comes back and wipes her face and hair... like he would a child, which she really still is. Her eyes do not leave the TV. He also takes a finger bowl of water, goes out to the doorsteps and scuds any sick away.

He returns to inspect her, reaches out and touches, clinically. one of her nipples. She reacts to its tenderness to that, all the time, though, having her eyes glued on the IPL replay)

NAVIN: You should come to the clinic today.
   (*then in Tamil*)
Neengal indru maruthuwa viduthi waravendum.

SHANTI: (in Tamil at first) Enna kaaranatrhitku? They cut off your furry little pussy there.

NAVIN: Mother is wrong, Shanti. You pop along.

SHANTI: Auntie wouldn't say if you was going to cut off my furry little pussy there, like all them others.

> *(The still-caring doctor, he goes to the sideboard, gets her a glass of water. She drinks it offhand, undistracted. He takes glass back, is fastidious to return it to is exact spot.*
>
> *Then he returns to the bed and covers himself totally from the world again. He is soon snoring again.*
>
> *In this silence of doing what she wants, the girl is delighted. She wriggles her toes, stretches luxuriously, throws 'ha!' gestures to cricketing villains, claps at heroes.*
>
> *Unfortunately, this doesn't last more than a few minutes.*
>
> *AUNTIE does her best to untangle herself from her baggy night dress to come flying out of the bedroom.)*

AUNTIE: Hey!

> *(As soon as the girl hears AUNTIE, she switches the TV off with the remote control with a practised one-fell-swoop, and dives under the bed.*
>
> *AUNTIE appears. Gaunt, bony, barely covered in a dirty old sleeveless nightie buttoned (wrongly) down the front which is revealing – and shockingly so, given her skeletal frame. (She wears this pretty much throughout, and just as carelessly)*

AUNTIE: (on the charge) Hey!, hey! You come here!

(She knows the girl is under the bed but any game of hide-and-seek there is going to be strongly weighted in favour of the girl. That doesn't matter; AUNTIE is set on catching the kid out and makes ludicrously arthritic attempts to corner and bend over to haul the child out. Finally, the old lady has to resort to going down on her knees, but this takes so long that the girl is able to slid out the other side unnoticed and get to the relative safety of the kitchen. There she stands in the doorway, all innocence, and watches tut-tutting as the old lady struggles up.

When the girl speaks, it is cocky and argumentative.... very inappropriate for a domestic help)

SHANTI: What? What?

AUNTIE: (struggling to get up) Hey!

SHANTI: What do you think you're doing?

AUNTIE: What am I doing, what am I doing? I'll give you what am I doing, you cheeky little moll! Is that water on?
   (*SHANTI turns her back, goes back into kitchen*)
Hey, you! I was talking to you! You come back!

   (SHANTI re-appears surlily)

SHANTI: Look at you down on your old knees like chicken elbows.

AUNTIE: I'll give you chicken elbows, you chickenfeed. I said no TV, no TV. I've had it with you.

SHANTI: (disingenuous whine) I was trying to switch it off, Auntie.

AUNTIE: Hey!, don't bull me, kiddo.

SHANTI: How would you know, see? You snoring away.

AUNTIE: I don't snore, I don't snore. You come here, you come right here!

> (The girl reluctantly goes up to her. AUNTIE grabs here with witch's glee and boney hands, then spins her around so she can inspect the form of the girl. She pats her on the bum, then pushes her hand against her belly, holding the other tight from squirming away.
>
> She pushes her away in disgust)

AUNTIE: I know what you are, don't think a smart old glamourpuss like me doesn't.

SHANTI: What, what now?

AUNTIE: Fetching up your quoit on my front doorstep, I heard you. That's my front doorstep, thank you very much. Being bilious.

SHANTI: Did not.

AUNTIE: You were bilious!

SHANTI: Me?

AUNTIE: (mimic) 'Me?' You don't even know what bilious is. Don't go coming the raw prawn with me, not with the Good Lord my provider. hallelujah.

> (The girl is not squirming, has to turn from AUNTIE and endeavours to hurry out.)

AUNTIE: (stopping her) Hey!, where do you think you're going?

SHANTI: (knees together, wanting toilet) To the hole.

AUNTIE: You're not going to the hole!

SHANTI: I'm allowed to go to the hole.

AUNTIE: You've just been to the hole.

SHANTI: I have not been to the hole.

AUNTIE: Hey!, you think I'm a mug? I'm Aussie, kiddo. I saw you sneaking a use of my potty, sneaky little buggerlugs, you.

(The girl gets away and still goes into AUNTIE's bedroom)

AUNTIE: I said no potty! That's the master bedroom, that is!

(In theory, AUNTIE should go about doing something else. But she doesn't; she waits until SHANTI finishes peeing – we hear it quite loudly, since she leaves the door open – and for the girl to come back out and face the inevitable music)

AUNTIE: (disgustedly) Use the flush.

SHANTI: (adjusting herself) What for?

AUNTIE: Hey!, we put paper between our hands and our bums in this house, or you go and use next door's garden. Honestly, peeing in a gal's pot and hawking up on her doorstep... what do ya think it is?

SHANTI: ('not me') I was sleeping.

AUNTIE: Bullsh. You were out here watching TV.

SHANTI: Oh, then.

AUNTIE: Yeah, then, then, Hey!, I said did you get that water on?

SHANTI: You never said anything about any water.

AUNTIE: Only every day! What's wrong with you? Right, that's it! You're gone. You're out. No mercy, no mercy. You get your driphead of a mother here to take you off.

SHANTI: She won't come here. Nobody wants to come here.

AUNTIE: She's taking you home today. No mercy, no mercy.

SHANTI: (now reverting to whining again) What about me? Nobody cares about me. You won't even let me watch some TV. You can snore away, but I've been up for hours and hours and hours working my fingers to the bone.

AUNTIE: Liar!

SHANTI: It's Sunday. Sundays, I'm always allowed to watch TV.

AUNTIE: TV? Your mob hasn't got a pot to pee in!

SHANTI: ('oh yeah?') We don't need the money. They only sent me here to get more English.

AUNTIE: Pull this one.

SHANTI: They didn't know you were Australian and I'd have to teach more English than I get.

AUNTIE: Hey, you watch it!

SHANTI: (stopping, curious) Watch what?

AUNTIE: (giving up) Let's see that water, you!

(She flusters out in the kitchen. The girl sullenly goes to

follow, but AUNTIE comes out again)

SHANTI: I did put that water on. It all boiled away, you snoring away.

AUNTIE: Liar, liar!

SHANTI: (real whine, indicating NAVIN) He said he wanted black tea. I don't know how to make black tea.

AUNTIE: Hey!, I've been trying to drive it into that thick skull of yours for months.

SHANTI: Nobody can know how to make black tea.

AUNTIE: Oh, yeah? Hey!, you tell me why, smarty pants.

SHANTI: Cause there's no such thing.
 (*scathingly at sleeping form of NAVIN*)
Black tea. What's he talking about?

AUNTIE: Don't you go getting too big for your breeches, young lady. That's your boss cockey there after I kakk it.

SHANTI: (whine) You want me to pour some tea in and then put water on, but, Auntie, what do you do with the milk?

AUNTIE: You don't put in the milk!

SHANTI: Oh, you've got to put in the milk. That's why my father breaks his back milking all those cows for.

AUNTIE: Your father wouldn't know how to bend his back, let alone break it.

SHANTI: No, really. What do you do with the milk?

AUNTIE: You think you're talking to a dumbcluck?

SHANTI: What's milk just sitting there?

AUNTIE: So what?

SHANTI: (shrewdly) Why do you have it delivered for then?

AUNTIE: Hey, ratbag! You're sending me to my grave, you are. Two months, two months going on ten years. This is the last time I'm showing you, get it?

> *(She grabs the girl and hauls her into the kitchen. But they can still be heard:)*

AUNTIE: Hey!, what're you doing? Who told you to touch the sugar?

SHANTI: You can't make tea without sugar, not in this day and age.

AUNTIE: Right, that's it! No mercy! You tell that droopy-drawers of a mother I want to see her.

SHANTI: (height of cheek) She's busy. It's Sunday, TV day.

AUNTIE: (shocked) Where the rotten water? Didn't you even do the pump?

SHANTI: I was too busy with the milk and sugar.

AUNTIE: Don't you go getting uppity with me. You get out there and start the pump...!

> *(They are heard going out the back door.*
>
> *There is a refreshing early Sunday morning quiet. From the bed, even with his head still covered comes a sigh of contentment from NAVIN.*
>
> *This is eventually broken by the noise of a three-wheeler*

outside and the re-entry of EKANAYAKE. He does so flustered in a gangly way. In the manner of his Sri Lankan race, he is smiling because things have gone terribly wrong, as though some bad thing has happened but he is not the cause of it... not directly at least. He speaks to the form of NAVIN, could not be expecting a reply)

EKANAYAKE: I missed her. Bloodypuckinghell.

AUNTIE: (somewhere off) Hey, watch your language!

EKANAYAKE: (obviously by now an automatic response) Sorry, Auntie. Did she come, Navin?

(AUNTIE pokes her head through the front door behind him)

AUNTIE: I'll have anyone's guts for garters swearing inside the house. This is the house of the Lord, hallelujah.

EKANAYAKE: Sorry, Auntie. But I was late for the plane of Dorothy's, blood....
  (*stops himself in time*)

AUNTIE: Hey!, there's no room for anybody else. All full up, all full up!

EKANAYAKE: (shout) Dorothy, Auntie.

NAVIN: (calls from under coverlet) Your daughter-in-law, Mother.

(AUNTIE waves EKANAYAKE over to her conspiratorially)

AUNTIE: I told that little moll, she goes today. I'm jack of it. Two months and she's still as silly as a hen in a wood-chopping comp.

EKANAYAKE: Is two months long enough, Auntie?

AUNTIE: No mercy, no mercy! Hey!, she still doesn't know how to make black tea.

EKANAYAKE: ('never heard of it') Black tea?

AUNTIE: Don't you start!
  (*she suddenly 'takes a shine' to him*)
You stay for lunch, you hear. I'll make you some nice rice and dahl curry. No, don't thank me now, just leave a big fat tip.

   (*She 'disappears' again. To talk to her, he has to follow*)

EKANAYAKE: You sure Dorothy didn't turn up, Auntie?

AUNTIE: (trips over something off) Ow!

   (*EKANAYAKE helps her back to the living room; she has stubbed her toe*)

AUNTIE: She left that lying there deliberately.
 (*pointing at NAVIN even though he is still under coverlet*)
You. You, buggerlugs. I hope you're satisfied. That little harpy's turning me hair white.
  (*gets no response, has to turn back to EKANAYAKE*)
Told you we're full up.

EKANAYAKE: Dorothy, Dorothy, Auntie. Your son David's wife. She's coming all the Australian way to talk to you.

AUNTIE: Hardly know the moll. More money than sense. She better not have fronted before a gal's had her morning cuppa. Need the heart starter or I'm no good for man or beast, telling you.
  (*grotesque coquettish eyes*)
And don't you go giving me them big old wolf's eyes, either, big boy.
  (*going towards kitchen, to NAVIN's form*)

You get up, buggerlugs and meet this Dorothy oojah. I'd go myself if I knew who she was, something about trying to worm her way into the family.

NAVIN: (muffled) She was here four months ago with David. David. Your son, Mother.

AUNTIE: Hey!, I know who my son David is. You be careful; I might ask you who you are.

NAVIN: (quite seriously) I'm your youngest. And please don't go blaming me again for that.

AUNTIE: (at EKANAYAKE) Lucky me.
   (*then plunging into kitchen*)
Hey!, Shanti!, what's going on? Where's the little galoot gone now...?

> (*After her, there is another long silence.*
>
> *At first, EKANAYAKE wonders whether he should go out again, but he opts to sit on settee and wait. Fortunately, this does not need to be long. A taxi pulls up outside. He jumps up, opens the door, hurries out.*
>
> *Eventually, DOROTHY enters. EKANAYAKE follows her with her bag. She has a sad smile on her face, which fades to a quizzical expression when there is no greeting.*
>
> *The Inspector shrugs apologetically)*

DOROTHY:
I see nothing's changed.
   (*then*)
Shit'n'sugar, I hate it when she does this!
   (*then, calming herself*)
Why sweat when it's only good for the prickly heat, right?

EKANAYAKE: Auntie is having a little trouble with the servant, isn't it?

DOROTHY: It's nice to see you again, Charles. Still over here watching the big bad Tamils?
 (*knowing she's only going to get a noncommittal shrug*)
That's Navin there, isn't it? Get up off your bum and say hello, Navin.

NAVIN: (graciously looking out) Dear lady, greetings, greetings. A little sleep in, Sundays, hmm?

DOROTHY: (back to EKANAYAKE) Please tell me she's changed a little bit.

NAVIN: (deciding to emerge) Hardly, dear Dorothy. I suppose we have the pleasure of your company because you're going to tell her about what really happened to David as against what the police briefly told us? Personally, I am wondering whether that's very wise, but I wouldn't want to be held to blame for what might seem to be an innocent bit of wondering on my side of things. What if Mother's already forgotten about it, we should be asking ourselves? Or not asking ourselves.

DOROTHY: Spray that again?

NAVIN: (confused himself) Pardon?
 (*then*)
Whatever point you're going to make, dear lady, I hope it doesn't involve a matter of any blame one way or the other. If so, I'll do my best to help you.

DOROTHY: That's as clear as mud, love, but thanks for the offer. Look, can someone sort of actually officially invite me in?

NAVIN: (irrespective) I don't know what David did or didn't do, but I do have a particularly good batch of ibufren in the car if you think Mother might need a mild pain killer.

DOROTHY: How much does she know?

NAVIN: I haven't asked, dear lady.

DOROTHY: Not even the little thing, like her eldest son murdered in his own driveway? No, I'm serious.

NAVIN: (wounded) I'm just trying to say that I hope there is no fault to lay at anyone's feet, meaning in this household far away from Australia, that's all.

DOROTHY: (long suffering) Navin, I need a brotherly kiss from you or they'll need a wheel barrel to carry my rejection.

> *(She almost has to heave him over to the side of the bed to get the quickest of pecks.)*

DOROTHY: Jesus, Navin, you're a doctor dealing with popping bellies day in and day out and you're blushing like a virgin.

NAVIN: Dental hygiene, dear lady. I haven't cleaned my teeth yet.

DOROTHY: Neither have I. A day and a half, at least, so top that. You couldn't believe what I've chewed and washed around in there.

> *(He quickly gets up -- he is wearing pyjamas impeccably -- and goes off to the bathroom. After he has gone, she has a good laugh with the Inspector. They are slightly interrupted by a series of 'hey's from AUNTIE somewhere off)*

DOROTHY: Am I going to have the same trouble getting through to her?
(then, indicating after NAVIN)
If I remember right, he'll only take a few minutes, max, but he'll be back all showered and shaved and dressed up like he'd been polished with Brasso. Don't ask me how he does it.

16

(*and*)
He still won't leave the nest, go out and get a wife, something?

EKANAYAKE: I suppose because this is India.

DOROTHY: Mummy's land.

EKANAYAKE: (amused at 'Mummy') 'Mummy'. Last week she got angry, wasn't it? That Time magazine was going to interview her as the foreigner living in the longest in India.

DOROTHY: (used to correcting him) 'Living the longest in India.' How long?

EKANAYAKE: I am not sure. Fifty years? More? Then they found some Italian priest who has been here six days longer than Auntie, or something just ...
   (*under breath*)
... bloodypuckinghell sorry like that.

DOROTHY: She would've gone up the wall. She learns where he lives, I wouldn't be that Italian priest for quids.
   (then appeal for any help possible)
Listen, Charlie, this time it's different. This time I've got to sit down and actually have a heart-to-heart with her but I've got no idea how to. See... I could never call her Auntie, and no way I'm calling her Mum. Shit'n'sugar, I can't even pronounce her proper name.... Sathiablahbloop... and I'm married to the bloody thing.

EKANAYAKE: Sathianathan.

DOROTHY: Yeah, yeah.
   (*thick tongue*)
Bloohblahblah.

EKANAYAKE: (suddenly) I grieved for you about your David.

   (She shudders thinking about it, goes to lift her overnight bag up onto the bed. He hurries to help her. All that

happens is they both let go at the same time and it falls onto the concrete floor and spills some content)

DOROTHY: There. See that mess in there? You should see inside my head.

(She sits down despondently on the bed)

EKANAYAKE: Would you like something? I think I could start with a cup of tea.

DOROTHY: Would I what.

EKANAYAKE: The trouble is getting something out of the kitchen these days, isn't it?

DOROTHY: A glass of water. Anything.

EKANAYAKE: A little matter of through the pump nothing, I think.
   (thankful alternative)
Maybe I am being able to buy from the shop for you.

DOROTHY: A glass of water from the shop? Look, I'll do it.
   (stops on way to kitchen)
Sorry, that was rude. I'll get it, thanks.

(But is diverted when NAVIN emerges from the bathroom, just as she said he would... that is, all showered, shaved and sprucely dressed, even though he's only been in there a few minutes and wasn't seen fetching clothes etcetera. He is drying one ear with a finger as a final touch)

DOROTHY: (at him) Quick-change artist. I'll never know how you do it, Navin.

NAVIN: (a new man) So, and how is my sister-in-law Dorothy? Oh, and how's that place whatsitcalled?

DOROTHY: Australia. There, satisfied? I let myself fall for it again.

NAVIN: Ha ha. And I'm fine, thanks. So's Mother. Except for poor David, of course. And my patients are fine. They're twenty per cent up on last year.

DOROTHY: Clever little dicks. Revenue too, huh?

NAVIN: Oh, nobody could dare call me a liar if I confessed to that being up over fifty per cent.

DOROTHY: Good strong growth. Just like...
   (*cueing him to old joke between them*)
the...

NAVIN: The bouncing babes I bring into the world, ha ha.

DOROTHY: The bouncing babes you bring into the world, ha ha.

NAVIN: I can't claim the blame for every one of them, ha ha.

DOROTHY: I hear tea and water's become a bit of a problem in India.

NAVIN: (suddenly serious again) Oh, I shouldn't be blame for that. I think it's better weekdays, though.

DOROTHY: Never mind, I'll brave it.

   (*She moves towards the kitchen again, but, as if by magic and certainly to her confusion, AUNTIE has instantly appeared to block her way*)

AUNTIE: Hey!

DOROTHY: (what else to say?) Hi!

AUNTIE: Need any help?

DOROTHY: It's Dorothy. You remember Dorothy?

NAVIN: She's still got a bit of trouble with a cataract or two.

AUNTIE: Who asked you, cock of the dung heap?
   (*to Dorothy about NAVIN*)
What can y'say about him? When I had him in the family way I knew he'd be in every dill's way.

EKANAYAKE: (to help out) You remember Dorothy ringing to say from Australia all the way she was coming in, Auntie.

AUNTIE: (indicating EKANAYAKE) Dumbclucks all round a sassy-little-something-even-like-me here. I sent him to meet you at the airport but did he cock it up? Hey!, he cocked it up. You show me good help you can rely on these days and I'll show you a bull with a bra.
   (*then conversationally*)
So. Lucky we're not full up. When did you get in?

DOROTHY: (confused yet again) This morning!

AUNTIE: Fly or what?

DOROTHY: (thoroughly depressed) I rang, no, I also alarm bells I was coming. About... David.

AUNTIE: Hey!, how's my boy Davie goin'? Copping a good screw now and again, is he?
   (*sees SHANTI sneaking away to the toilet again*)
Hey!, hey!, what're you doing, dopey?

SHANTI: Going to the hole, so there.

AUNTIE: Going to the hole, my bum. You get your mind off that hole and you get your hole back into that kitchen or you're gone. No mercy, no mercy!

(She swings back into the kitchen, grabs SHANTI on the way. SHANTI grabs DOROTHY to stop herself being dragged away. AUNTIE and DOROTHY have a tug of war over the girl, until the girl lets go of DOROTHY and lets herself be pulled into the kitchen... apparently to the fridge)

AUNTIE: (off) Hey!, you get away from the fridge! You get your thieving little mitts outa there. I know where they've been!
   (and just as suddenly is out talking to DOROTHY again.)
You could be right about David, Dot. You take that...
   (indicates NAVIN)
... useless tall streak of water there, you take my two daughters. They're in Canada and their hubbies're getting really good screws more often'n'not, so it goes to show what regular nooky does. I've lived in this house fifty-six years with the good Lord.... God is Great, hallelujah!... and my two daughters in Canada are always giving their old Mum a good tingle. Any pay rise their hubbies get, guess who's the first to know? Hey!, every time I ask was it the screw and they say wasn't it ever! If David was getting the right screw I'd be the first to know. You two got any children or anything?

DOROTHY: (in desperation) We were only here a couple of months ago. Do I look pregnant?

AUNTIE: (snorts) Aussie sheilas. Useless in the pit!
   (indicates over shoulder to kitchen)
I know what that one is, too. Hey!, my grandchildren are going to uni. They're into soft wires or something.

NAVIN: Software, Mother.

AUNTIE: (ignoring him) Tell you what, you have any snot noses back home what could mate with my grandkids in America?

NAVIN: Canada, Mother.

AUNTIE: You write down their names and I'll send your request on. But no syph. I won't have syph in the family. Bad enough those weak chests got in a couple of times. So, you after more tea or something?

DOROTHY: I haven't had the first one yet.

AUNTIE: Didn't they give you one on the plane? I'd be asking a refund if it was me.

DOROTHY: I had coffee on the plane.

AUNTIE: There you go then. You've got to be happy with what you've got.
   (and yet:)
So, what's in your tea?

DOROTHY: Black?

AUNTIE: Hey!, don't you start.

   (but she returns to the kitchen anyway)

DOROTHY: (near shout after her) Maybe we can have a little talk and I can be on my way tomorrow, if that's all right.
   (but no answer)
Shit'n'sugar!

AUNTIE: (off) Hey!, no swearing round here!

DOROTHY: Sorry, sorry.

   (But she mouths 'shit'n'sugar' again.

   It is SHANTI who this time re-emerges. She stands in the doorway, her arms crossed and her head at a quizzing angle. There is nothing of servitude in her manner:)

SHANTI: Neengal eppadi calffee edupeer gal?

NAVIN: She's asking you how you have your coffee.

DOROTHY: What happened to the tea? Look, as long as it's wet. (*to girl*)
Black.

SHANTI: (possibly deliberate over-familiarity) Black? Your man didn't have it black.

AUNTIE: (re-appearance) Hey!, what's going on?

> *(SHANTI suddenly doubles over in pain. At first they think it theatrics but her distress is real)*

NAVIN: (nonchalantly taking over) Just a touch of hyperemesis. Common amongst teenage girls.

DOROTHY: Not the teenage girls I know!

NAVIN: Teenage girls of India. But we mustn't lay blame helter-skelteredly, when a few handy ibufren could be just the ticket.

AUNTIE: (over the girl and showing concern, despite:) Skulker, skulker.

SHANTI: (pathos) Need the hole, Auntie.

AUNTIE: You've just been to the hole! Hey!

NAVIN: I would recommend the hole, Mother.

AUNTIE: Pull on this; it'll sing Dixie!

SHANTI: (instantly 'cured' anyway) It's your old-lady cooking.

AUNTIE: Hey!, I'll give you old-lady cooking, you little moll! You come here.

> *(She drags the girl off into the kitchen. Pause.)*

DOROTHY: Forget the shit'n'sugar. Make that shit-a-brick.

AUNTIE: (off) Hey!

DOROTHY: (drily) Yeah, sorry.

   (She gives up, plops down on the bed.)

DOROTHY: My memory's shot. I should have remembered how hard this would be.
(then a thought)
That kid of a girl, god, she's not all duffed up, is she, Navin?
(to his brief nod)
She's too young even for India, right?

NAVIN: (quite sternly for him) She's really quite healthy, dear lady. Personally, I have been hoping our Charles here would do the policeman's thing and query the girl's parents and their cousins. He's very good at avoiding machetes.

EKANAYAKE: (alarmed) Me?

NAVIN: Dorothy, would you say that that was a cri de coeur? I think I would, definitely.

EKANAYAKE: Why me all the time?

NAVIN: Now, was that a cri de coeur?

   (AUNTIE shows herself again)

AUNTIE: Hey!, it's easy for some to say black tea or then change their mind to black coffee.

DOROTHY: (very wearily) Milk and sugar in whatever's fine by me.

AUNTIE: Now the dopey little moll's gone and spilt the milk.

EKANAYAKE: I'll go down the shop, Auntie.

AUNTIE: (slyly) Somebody's knocked over the sugar too.

EKANAYAKE: I'll get sugar, too.

AUNTIE: (craftily) What'd you be using for moolah?

> *(He stops hopefully. But no one volunteers. They turn their eyes on DOROTHY, who sighs, opens handbag, then has to:)*

DOROTHY: Oh God, I've forgot to get my money changed.

AUNTIE: (mumble) Hey!, pull this one.

> *(Suddenly, there is a tile-smashing crash on the roof.*
>
> *After the initial shock, EKANAYAKE, NAVIN and DOROTHY run out to see what it was. AUNTIE and the girl noticeably hurry to each other for comfort.*
>
> *The others return)*

NAVIN: It's all right.

DOROTHY: What sort of whack throws a brick on a tiled roof?

EKANAYAKE: (talking it down) I'll get a tomorrow someone to fix it.

DOROTHY: 'Someone tomorrow'. What is it, smashing roofs the latest in India? I prefer back home's pinging the unemployed.

EKANAYAKE: (bringing it back to 'normal') I'll get that milk and sugar.

> *(He leaves as an excuse to look around outside more closely)*

AUNTIE: (opportunistically after him:) And rice. And some nice new dahl. Potatoes. And grapes. No ikkies on them like last time or you'll be taking them back, I'm sick of it.
 (*she turns back into room*)
Hey!, is that man going to be long? I haven't had my morning brew yet.
 (*as if she has just noticed her*)
Hey!

DOROTHY: (shocked into.) Hey!

AUNTIE: What's it like back home in Oz? Still shitty?

> (*She sits in a plastic child's chair by the lounge table, cups one knee in her hands and leans back in a grotesque cheesecake pose. In her flimsy nightie, this is very revealing and very revolting, such that both DOROTHY and NAVIN have to avert their eyes. However, she is on for a 'real good' conversation*)

AUNTIE: So was the train late again, that's what did the corners of your mouth?

DOROTHY: Train? I honestly don't know.

AUNTIE: Call me Auntie or call me up sometime. And how's my David doing? Doing all right but not as good as his sisters in Canada, that the drift? Hey!, what do I call you apart from Dorothy.
 (*snorts*)
I've come across a few Dorothys in my time, phew whiff. Dot dot dot...

> (*She jumps up, launches herself back into the kitchen. As she goes:*).

AUNTIE: Hey!, slackie, you get off that big khyber of yours and put the water on.

DOROTHY: (finally, ironic) Alone at last.

NAVIN: (fateful prospect) Does this mean we're going to talk?

DOROTHY: Anything's possible, brother-in-law.

NAVIN: No, I mean. Should I have prepared for something verbal? It's just that I ought to be leaving before any finger-pointing starts.

DOROTHY: (not worth answering) Has she registers anything at all about David?

NAVIN: I really wouldn't know.

DOROTHY: You know, somebody should look after that kid. She's real survivor stuff. Around here, she needs to be.

NAVIN: She was the only one I could get. I can't be blamed if no one will work for Mother anymore.

DOROTHY: Have I been wrong. Does your mother even want to hear about David?

NAVIN: I do. At least I did before I come to think about it

DOROTHY: Meaning?

(He picks up the morning paper, sits to ostensibly glance over it)

DOROTHY: Jesus, Navin.

NAVIN: (all innocence) Hmm?

DOROTHY: I don't get how you can keep living here.

NAVIN: Oh, I couldn't move, you know. There's my practice.

DOROTHY: You're operating from here now?

NAVIN: No, but my patients have got to be able to contact me in emergencies.

DOROTHY: What about your mobile phone?

NAVIN: Pardon me?

DOROTHY: Your mobile. Like, it doesn't matter where you are.

NAVIN: But what has that got to do with not living here?

DOROTHY: Navin, love, forget I asked.

NAVIN: I hope I haven't offended you already.

DOROTHY: No.

NAVIN: I wouldn't want to think I'm responsible for doing that.

DOROTHY: You not.

NAVIN: It wouldn't look too good to my patients.

> *(She is almost relieved when AUNTIE comes back. But even this becomes disjointing when the old lady comes close to her, grabs her hand and starts patting the back of it.*
>
> *They remain like that as if frozen in time. Only after a long and painful silence)*

AUNTIE: So, so?
 (*waits smilingly for an answer, is unperturbed not getting one*) Don't let anyone come to think they can throw their leg over you, girlie. Hey!, they're always after bits of skirts like us. How many times do I have to tell you, dummy?

(Dreamily, she lets DOROTHY's hand go and drifts over to her bedroom. In sight in there, she puts a dirty old towel on her head as a scarf and then proceeds to do her praying.

Her praying consists of the dynamic type -- new Baptism -- during which she is supposed to dance around in praise, but, with her age, actually shuffles forwards and sideways, with little hops in between. While doing this she is constantly mumbling 'God is Great, Jesus is the Lord. Hallelujah'.

In the middle of this, SHANTI slips out from the kitchen, dives for a corner of the bed. She slithers under the bed to the other side and emerges to use the remote to switch on the TV. Its burst of noise doesn't matter to her; she watches and animates the cricket replay while trying to stop herself from going again 'to the hole'.

Only finally does it get to AUNTIE. She breaks off her praying and heads to switch off the TV)

AUNTIE: Hey!, what'd I say?! Right, you come here!

(The girl scuttles back under the bed and they repeat the earlier hide-and-seek routine of earlier, until SHANTI can make a dash for the kitchen on her hands and knees.

Eventually, dirty towel still on head, she realises that no one is under the bed. She looks suspiciously at DOROTHY)

DOROTHY: Don't look at me.

(AUNTIE launches herself back into the kitchen)

AUNTIE: Hey!, that's it! No mercy, no mercy! You finish that work, then you're clocking out.

SHANTI: (disdainfully) 'Clocking out'. What's that mean?

AUNTIE: I'll clock you one, you pipsqueak!

DOROTHY: (finally to NAVIN) Don't get me wrong, but wouldn't you say she's finally gone off her tit?

NAVIN: (folding up paper, prepares to leave) Well, another day, another rupee, ha ha. My mothers-to-be know no Sabbaths, dear lady.

> *(but is obviously in no hurry to leave, especially now that EKANAYAKE returns with his load of groceries, shrugs to them 'What to do?', goes off into the kitchen, dropping an advertising leaflet on the coffee table near her as he goes)*

DOROTHY: Junk mail on Sundays? India's looking up.

> *(NAVIN takes up the leaflet with loving care)*

NAVIN: I wouldn't quite call it junk mail since it could be suspected as my own junk mail. Don't tell Mother but I slipped it into the letter box last night. What do you think?

> *(But he doesn't share the flyer anyway, only checks it over admiringly himself, then places it on the coffee table in pride of place)*

DOROTHY: Business must be good, I see. Flyers about floating foetuses and whathaveyou.

NAVIN: Statistics tell us India is always on the up-and-up when making babies, don't you know.

DOROTHY: Yeah, I noticed a brand new yellow Mercedes in the driveway. Congrats.

NAVIN: It's good to have one's patients know who's coming, dear lady. Yellow was voted the number one your-gynaecologist-is-coming colour, don't you know. I think I can take the blame for starting that survey. As I told David, a few more percentage points on the od turnover and I could even be looking at giving up the morgue.

DOROTHY: Ah, yes, I'd forgotten about the morgue. How's the morgue, Navin? Business looking up there, too?

NAVIN: A little moonlighting, don't you know, as Assistant Medical Officer, A.D.M.O., Coroner really, of all south Chennai. But it's hard giving up the initials after the name, ya?
   (*then*)
Actually, that's where I'm off to now.
   (*then conspiratorially*)
Bit of an emergency. Four more eyes... phfttt!.... gone Friday night. I'll bet you they're going to lay the blame at my feet.

DOROTHY: Eyes. Pfftttt.

NAVIN: Pfftttt.

DOROTHY: What's pfftttt?

   (They are incredibly interrupted again by AUNTIE bursting in from out of the kitchen, making straight for DOROTHY)

AUNTIE: David. Good hubby? In the cot, keeps you all calmed down, did he? Hey!, plenty of....
   (copulating movement which is ludicrous and lewd)
how's-your-father? I did with mine. No waiting around wondering where the next whoo-whoo was coming from. A real animal that man was. He wouldn't believe what I've got to put up with in...
   (meaning SHANTI in the kitchen)
there. Hey!, it's alright for you but who's got time to think of jiggy-jigs on your r mind and nothing else/

DOROTHY: It was only tea or coffee.

   (There is an almost inevitable smashing of crockery in the kitchen. AUNTIE dashes off)

AUNTIE: Hey!, myxo-head, whatareya, whatareya?

(The instance she enters the kitchen, EKANAYAKE manages to escape from it. By his expression, it could have been a real war zone)

EKANAYAKE: Bloodypuckinghell sorry.

AUNTIE: (off) Hey!

EKANAYAKE: Sorry, sorry, Auntie.

DOROTHY: Hell in there, is it?

EKANAYAKE: And they call it a civilian zone.

(He joins her on the bed. Finally:)

DOROTHY: Join us in a conversation about eyes going ppfftttt in the night.

NAVIN: Well, you know the morgue, Charles.

DOROTHY: Four eyes. One night. Pfftttt.

NAVIN: (sagely) All four. AWOL. The trouble is, we did have a hydraulic dissecting table once but it's now sitting on wooden blocks that are more termite proof but wobbles just as much unfortunately. We had a generator for lighting around ten years ago, but someone disconnected the power lines, but we do have two petromax lamps. But personally I prefer doing my autopsies by candlelight; there's no need to bar a bit of a romantic setting just because it is a morgue, that's what I feel if nobody objects to me feeling that. There's a few torches, but they take the batteries with all the backyard cricket the night shift gets up to. Air conditioning, ditto the power lines. So you see the problem, don't you?

   (stops for appreciation but doesn't wait for it)

You can see how we are obliged to store our .... customers outside under the Neem tree there. Lots of branches, lots of shade. And Neem keeps the mosquitoes off, don't you know. The trouble is there's always some rush, rush, rush. Like, last week, that bus accident and all those primary schoolers. We were flooded out, I don't mind telling you.

(*petulantly*)

There were far more eyes taken that night than my watch last Friday night so I don't know what's the big kerfuffle about my miserly four. And by the way, I wouldn't want you to blame me personally for our customers being left uncovered. Personally, I could never believe those crows and those mice and those palm cats and the bandicoots can be such persistent little beggars. Face them with an eye and you can forget all about the colonial concept of fair crack of the whip.

DOROTHY: Shit'n'sugar.

NAVIN: The cockroaches are the worst in my opinion, but please don't quote me on that. Off with the soft fleshes around the eyes and nose and ears and, well, even more disgusting parts than those, and they think it's simply wonderland.

DOROTHY: Should we all start to throw up?

(NAVIN laughs quite merrily. Makes his way to the door, and as a happy parting gesture)

NAVIN: (calls) I'm off, Mother.

AUNTIE: (off) Good riddance.

DOROTHY: Charlie-horse, I've got a suspicion you know more than me about David anyway.
\
EKANAYAKE: Interpol, online. But no more than you, nae?

DOROTHY: Have you said anything to Auntie or Navin?

EKANAYAKE: (shocked) No.

DOROTHY: Why not? You're the cop. You must be used to laying it all out.

EKANAYAKE: Never. Not with Auntie.

DOROTHY: You think Navin's right? That it's best to leave it all alone?

(He can't answer. Silence between them)

DOROTHY: God, one moment it's crashing around like a Bondi tram in here, the next you're in the Simpson Desert. Where do they go?

EKANAYAKE: I sometimes am wondered by that myself.

DOROTHY: 'I sometimes wonder about that myself'.
   (*indicating the kitchen*)
It's like the black hole of Calcutta in there.

> *(She makes a decision, strides into the kitchen, makes it through without AUNTIE blocking her way... a cause for her to give him a grinning thumbs up.*
>
> *Now it is his turn to look lonely.*
>
> *It is only a short time that he has to sit there alone, though. SHANTI hurries in through the front door this time.*
>
> *Somehow she has gotten hold of AUNTIE's chamber pot. She makes for the TV, places the pot on the floor near the bed and, hitching up her skirt, squats on it. From here, she manages to do mimicry of the IPL replays. She is in bliss.*
>
> *EKANAYAKE watches her with fascination)*

EKANAYAKE: Should I be regarding you as a study of a growing criminal mind?

SHANTI: Ssh!

EKANAYAKE: (mockingly) So sorry, missy.

> *(But, sure enough, AUNTIE flusters in from the front door too)*

AUNTIE: Hey!, you little bugger! No TV, no TV!

> *(shapes to hit her, but really without intention; and, anyway, the girl takes no notice)*

SHANTI: He was watching it, not me.

AUNTIE: Liar! You pack your bag!

SHANTI: Who's got a bag? You have to pay me for me to get a bag.

AUNTIE: (to EKANAYAKE who is trying to keep out of this) Did this cheeky little harpy say something about pay?

SHANTI: You never pay me, you old woman you.

EKANAYAKE: Don't talk like that, girlie.

> *(... while AUNTIE nearly has apoplexy. She makes for her bedroom, deflated because she realises she has been caught out; the girl is right about the pay. She closes the bedroom door behind her.*
>
> *SHANTI claps with triumph, returns to the TV, even turns sound up and settles in for the watching long haul.*
>
> *But AUNTIE is not down and out as much as she imagines. She comes back out, switches off the set, goes back to*

bedroom, slamming the door behind him..

As soon as she does so, SHANTI goes to turn it back on.)

EKANAYAKE: (surprising authority) No, you don't. Get on with your work.

(The girl jumps with the command, but shows cockiness by controlling herself to walk with silly dignity out of the front door, pouring out the chamber pot just outside and in plain view of him. She blows him a raspberry.

AUNTIE has been watching this somehow. As soon as the girl leaves, she comes out of the bedroom, crosses to the sideboard and pulls a long glass of yellowish looking water from a jug. This she takes over to EKANAYAKE as a reward. He is trying to hide himself in the morning paper, but she still stands at his side, pushing the glass sideways so it keeps nudging his arm)

AUNTIE: (finally) Drink.

EKANAYAKE: No thanks, Auntie.

AUNTIE: Drink, drink.
   (knowing he has to, he drinks a little and hands it back. But she keeps nudging it against his arm)
Drink, drink.

   (Finally he is obliged to drink it all down.

   When he hands back the glass, she returns it to the sideboard and takes pains to position (although not to wash) the glass where it came from. Having done that, she goes over to the kitchen doorway -- where SHANTI has returned from around the back to stand to watch the 'drink,

drink' episode -- and stands 'over' the girl in a triumph of who's-boss which perhaps only they can understand)

AUNTIE: Come, come. Bring the hole.

(The girl follows her meekly back into the bedroom. {She will sleep on the floor at AUNTIE's feet as customary.}

AUNTIE is just closing the door when NAVIN returns; she waits for his inevitable greeting)

NAVIN: (but first quickly to EKANAYAKE) Don't blame me if I forget my head one day.
 (*then*)
It's only me, Mother.

AUNTIE: Who cares?

(and closes the bedroom door in his face.

This deflates NAVIN. He looks to EKANAYAKE for some sympathy, gets none. Sits on the bed miserably. Finally:)

NAVIN: Charles, you're fulltime, in a manner of speaking, where I'm really only part-time in the official realm, you know.

EKANAYAKE: (closing paper) What is it?

NAVIN: Well, just say you had the care of some eyes, four to be exact, and come Saturday morning, you are informed that same said eyes seemed to have flown the coop, don't you know. And say the living family of the missing eyes, quite dead now, mind you, and them, the family, not even Christian as far as one can see, well, they might be demanding an eye for an eye.
 (*panics*)
They might go all silly and sue!

EKANAYAKE: What can I do?

NAVIN: Being a policeman, don't you know. You could surely know a few growling types who pay visits along the lines of warning shots...?

EKANAYAKE: Don't even think about it.

NAVIN: But you will?

EKANAYAKE: *No!*

> *(Fortunately DOROTHY wanders back from the kitchen with a cup of something hot in her hand)*

DOROTHY: I'd offer you one, but it'd take the enamel off your teeth.

NAVIN: (defensively) We were only talking about missing parts.

EKANAYAKE: What's the loss of average rate for a night, anyway?

NAVIN: (hopefully) Oh, two at the outside! Four's nothing really.

DOROTHY: Ah, the eyes that pfffttt in the night, eh?

NAVIN: Charles was unblamefully discussing what we were going to do about them.

EKANAYAKE: I wouldn't be saying 'we'.

DOROTHY: (amused) Were they covered? Who's to blame if somebody should've covered them?

NAVIN: (desolate) We certainly used to cover them, but it was running up the laundry bill no end. A drain on the overheads, you see.
> (*histrionically*)

Did that matter to me? It did not! With these own hands, in a proxy sense, I put bricks over their faces and I distinctly remember those children with the four eyes being two of the recipients. They were fresh bricks.
   (*gets no response*)
Fresh *clean* bricks.
   (*miserably*)
It's this damnable mating season. It makes a cockroach think he's out of Bollywood.

   (Now the Inspector and DOROTHY look at each other and start to giggle. They can't help:)

EKANAYAKE: Well, Navin, I advise when you see coming parents at you, you should find a pile of nice fresh clean bricks and

DOROTHY and EKANAYAKE in unison: … hide under them!

   (They burst out into open laughter at him)

NAVIN: Don't blame me if I thought I could turn to you two for help.

DOROTHY: Tell you what, Navin lovie. You tell me where you got Holy Terror in there from and I'll throw in an idea.

NAVIN: (settles happily back) I think I can lay claim to rescuing her. The girl is next door help's first born, you see, and the woman was going to pop her off to the temple for a fate worse than death, don't you know.

DOROTHY: What's wrong with that, apart from her eating the temple paintwork?

NAVIN: (loadedly) They used to call them temple dancers. Nowadays, they don't pretend they dance. I am not the originator of that story.

DOROTHY: You're kidding. She's just out of diapers.

NAVIN: Helps the parents afford a new fridge or something, you see. The only flubble is, I tend to think, the temple's likely to throw them out maybe around sixteen at the stage of which they can't really go home, don't you know. Then perhaps they've got only the streets.

DOROTHY: (clap-hands) My brother-in-law Navin's a Hindu hero!

NAVIN: (demurely) One little girl out of tens of thousands, dear lady.

DOROTHY: Not the girl. I'm talking about the living hell you saved the temple priests from.

NAVIN: (catching up) Oh. Ha, ha.

DOROTHY: (but turning sour) On that 'flubble' business of yours… the kid's only recently pregnant, though, right?
   (*he hesitates; she repeats*)
This wasn't no temple's fault, right?

NAVIN: (at her glare) I hope you're not blaming me.

EKANAYAKE: (hardnosed on the news-to-him) Who should we be looking at?

NAVIN: (struggling for composure) No no no. The father, one of the brothers, one of the uncles, who knows? Don't be looking at me!

DOROTHY: She'd hardly be old enough for the bleeds.

NAVIN: (firmer ground) Karma, dear lady.

DOROTHY: Look, I've told you before don't give me that! You can't seriously be telling me that if she's out of here into the street it's her karma.

NAVIN: I'm afraid we can't do anything about Karma, dear lady. Isn't it so, Charles?

(The Inspector turns his face away, but doesn't deny it)

DOROTHY: Shit'n'sugar.

NAVIN: All's karma, Dorothy. But, as I said, I think, let's wait and see.

(There is a sudden loud snoring from the bedroom. It is so loud, it is embarrassing, a conversation stopper)

NAVIN: (weak laugh) Mother. My karma.

(Still refusing to get off the warpath, DOROTHY picks up the advertising leaflet which NAVIN is so proud about. She is scathing as she reads it aloud)

DOROTHY: 'Don't Disappoint!' Exclamation mark. 'Take home what your husband fancies. Population controlled. Proven gynaecological sneak previews!' Exclamation mark. 'Full correctional facilities. Ultrasound Ultrasound Ultrasound' ... three 'Ultrasounds', two exclamation marks... 'lookings into very closely. 800 rupees nearly all-inclusive. The 8 crossed out and a nine handwritten over it. The Happier Dad Baby Clinic. Address:....' etc etc. Oh, and 'PS: ask for our Viagra discounts' three exclamation marks.
  (*then at NAVIN*)
The Happier Dad Baby Clinic.

NAVIN: I could be enticed into admitting thinking up that common touch.

(The bedroom door is pushed open and SHANTI emerges, hair all tossled from a deep nap. She walks groggily over to the TV, covering her ears theatrically from AUNTIE's snoring. She takes no notice of the adults watching her, as

she sits among them and switches on the TV. It is a Hindi movie.

The others know she is not going to get away with it, and watch with a great deal of expectation. Sure enough, AUNTIE emerges sleep bedraggled)

AUNTIE: Hey! Hey!

(The girl dives under the bed and, unnoticed by the old woman, again scrambles along the floor to make the sanctuary of the kitchen.

Not finding the girl where she expected to confuses AUNTIE. She turns to the others:)

AUNTIE: Who turned on the idiot box? No TV! A gal's trying to get some beauty sleep around here.

(As some sort of ritual punishment, she crosses to the sideboard, fills up two glasses of yellowy water from the pitcher and brings them back to NAVIN and EKANAYAKE. She puts them down beside the men and waves at the glasses)

AUNTIE: Drink, drink.

(Neither of them want to, and at first make no movement to do so, but she stays rock-like by them, obviously not going to be moved until her will is done.

NAVIN motions that they'd better do it. She only stops intoning when they have finished it all:)

AUNTIE: Drink, drink.

(Then when they have, she takes the glasses back to the sideboard and neatly puts them back into their places. Stands there sleepily looking at the glasses, while:)

DOROTHY: Speaking of which, where can I get a couple of bottles of mineral water?

AUNTIE: (automatic, indicating EKANAYAKE) He'll get it.

EKANAYAKE: (meekly) I'll go and get it.

AUNTIE: (coming to life with the cunning of it all) And my biscuits and the almond choccies.
  (to others)
He'd forget his head if it wasn't screwed on.
  (heads back into kitchen)
Hey! Shanti! You cleaned that rice yet?

SHANTI: (off) What rice?

AUNTIE: Hey!, don't try pretending dopey in this house, dopey, or the steel toecaps of me hobnails right up your flue, right? You get that rice cleaned quicksmart, or smat!, that's the sound of your slack bum hitting the deck.

SHANTI: Old woman!

AUNTIE: Hey!, hey! Don't go getting too big for your breeches, Miss bulging-in-front...

EKANAYAKE: (at DOROTHY) Two bottles, was it?

DOROTHY: You're an angel, you know that?

> *(He leaves for the shop, not at all sorry to be getting out of there. It gives DOROTHY the chance to get back to the wording of the leaflet in order to get at NAVIN)*

DOROTHY: Who's the genius at exclamation marks?

> *(But she can only groan aloud when AUNTIE yet again appears all sweetness and light. She leans on DOROTHY's*

shoulder, carries on conversationally as though nothing had interrupted her greeting DOROTHY's arrival)

AUNTIE: So you hoofed it all the way from Australia just to see me. The cops onto you or something?

DOROTHY: I'm your daughter-in-law.

AUNTIE: Pull this one, I know that.
   (*at NAVIN*)
What's wrong with her?

DOROTHY: (now angry) I came here to tell you about David, remember?

AUNTIE: (suddenly) Stand aside, Madam Mountain coming through!

(She shoves the dirty towel on her head again, starts her dynamic praying again.... 'God is Great. Jesus is Lord. Hallelujah' etc. They simply have to get out of her way.

DOROTHY goes to the window; NAVIN dodges artfully where he is. But, surprisingly, the old woman finishes her praying when she thinks of something, sidles out to DOROTHY's side again)

AUNTIE: So, whatdya think of the old Blue Boys, how're they going, like a steam train?

DOROTHY: Beg yours?

AUNTIE: The Blue Boys, the Blue Boys. Hey!, Carlton. *Whatareya?* Some ignoramus outa dopey Sydney? You ever seen my Blue Boys! Talk about specimens! Thighs on 'em like my Aunt Nellie and she used to stand in for the bullock working the plough, tellingya. You take that Grand Final I dragged my old man along to in Sixty-something. Against those ratbags Collingwood it was.

(*spits*)
Hey!, stripes on 'em ought to be yellow, tell me about it. Gawd love me Blue Boys, we didn't win, we shit in. My man was jealous over me n' the boys for a whole week and didn't he ever need to be. Tellingya.

NAVIN: I think that's enough, Mother!

AUNTIE: (eyes heavenwards) Dispensation, dispensation!
(*then*)
Look at that Don Bradman. I called him The Don. What a full forward that man was! Up there Cazaly had nothing on that killer-diller. A jock strap like it was filled with rocks that only he could shake a stick at. You shoulda seen his torpedo.
(*then*)
You two had breakfast?

DOROTHY: (hopefully) No, actually.

AUNTIE: (magnanimously) Come, come.
(*shouts to kitchen*)
Hey!, Shanti!, you get your smelly little twat out here and set the table!

> *(With surprising efficiency, SHANTI does emerge and she and the old lady get the table quite nicely set up with tablecloth, dish mats and so forth. Bread, butter, jug of water. And so:)*

AUNTIE: Come come come come come.

NAVIN: (excusing himself) I'm late, Mother.

AUNTIE: You come or, flump!, you'll cop a knuckle sandwich.

> *(The two are obliged to move to the table, where, again surprisingly, the old lady holds the chairs out for each of them. When they are seated, she stands over them, and pours each a glass of 'that' water. Then she tears off two*

hunks of bread from the loaf and literally throws -- though not intentionally -- them onto their plates. She gouges out two lumps of butter and plonks these down next to the bread. Then she stands back proudly, hovers around)

AUNTIE: Eat, eat.
>*(with her finger, she shoves DOROTHY's piece of bread closer on the plate to her)*

Fill your slack guts. Tonight we're having some nice rice and dahl curry. I'm cooking. Sometimes a gal gets tired of just being a pretty face; know what I mean?
>*(but she is distracted that the girl is alone in the kitchen)*

Hey!, Shanti!, what're you doing in there?
>*(going)*

Wherever it is, you knock it off or I'll do you…!

>*(She leaves 'administering' their eating, goes to find out what is going on in the kitchen)*

DOROTHY: (to NAVIN) Is this all? Bread and butter?!

NAVIN: (whisper) She's forgotten the curry.
>(*then, opportunistic too*)

You were going to give me an idea for my little 'pffftttt' embarrassment.

DOROTHY: (a promise's a promise) I was just thinking maybe you should hop into the local toy shop, pick up four marbles and you could dinky back to the morgue and sellotape them in.

NAVIN: (lighting up) Brilliant!

DOROTHY: Tombola size I'd reckon. Check out the colours. Maybe mix'n'match. Go the trendy.

>*(She takes her chunk of bread over to the front door and heaves it outside. Returns to sit forlornly on the bed.*
>
>*Dutifully, NAVIN tries to get his piece down, but is*

extremely quick to leave the table when the phone rings.

Even so, it becomes a mini-race between him and his mother to reach the receiver. He wins, but she hovers at his side impatiently)

NAVIN: Yes. Yes, that's right. Me? I'm Doctor Navin Sathianathan. Yes, yes, I am my mother's son. Excuse me, enough of the contradictions; are you having regular contractions? What? Oh, I do beg your pardon.

AUNTIE: (at him) Hey!, whosit, whosit?

NAVIN: (fierce whisper) It's Time magazine. The Indian edition.

AUNTIE: What a rag!

NAVIN: (back onto phone) Really. Really? Really? This coming Wednesday… ten o'clock. Oh, don't worry; I can be here holding her hand, ha ha. Of course. Have you got a pen and paper? Ha ha of course you do, Time magazine ha ha. Doctor Navin S. P. Sathianathan, gynaecologist and Assistant Coroner. You can also ask about me at the very very popular The Happier Dad Baby Clinic. I can send you an advertising leaflet. Very many Specials of the Day.
   (*is obviously cut off, shouts down receiver*)
We'll have our own website soon!
   (*puts receiver down, is excited*)
Time magazine, Mother!

AUNTIE: I'm ain't baring m'self for any centrefold.

NAVIN: No, no. You're It, Mother. The foreigner in all India living here the longest! The Italian priest died!

AUNTIE: ('explains it') Catholic, was he? Weak as water, Catholics. No mick's ever held out longer'n five minutes in the sack.

NAVIN: No, no. The Catholic priest. He was Number One. Now you're Number One Longest Indian Liver!

AUNTIE: (clapping hands) Hey!, that old coot kakked it?

NAVIN: Yes!

AUNTIE: Make way for the world champeen! Madam Mountain comin' through!
  (*does a parody of a gig*)
Tonight we celebrate, right, Dot y'old poor-man's pussy?

DOROTHY: (dully) Rice and dahl curry, goodie.

AUNTIE: Too bloody right!
  (*and*)
Hey!, Shanti!, you get off that lazy little fanny and get that water on! Tonight's the night! The sky's the limit! Up the Mighty Blue Boys!
  (*singing*)
Down behind the GPO, parlez vous
Down behind the GPO, parlez vous
Down behind the GPO, I kissed the girl and she gave me the pox.
Inky pinky parlez vous.

(end Act 1)

Act 2

(It is now late afternoon/early evening.

The household is having its afternoon nap, but the central bed is empty.

Incongruously, though, the front door has been left open. Outside we hear a three-wheeler taxi rev up. Then a man walks in unhurriedly. He is wearing a balaclava over his head. He props an envelope up on the lounge table, takes the TV and then casually walks out with it.

The three-wheeler takes off.

Long pause.

AUNTIE's bedroom door opens and SHANTI comes out rubbing sleep from her eyes. She makes for the door, too sleepy to notice it is open, hitching up her skirt to go to 'the hole' obviously just outside the front door.

When she soon returns, she automatically makes for the remote control, sits on the floor, makes herself comfortable, then points the remote control at the vacant spot where the TV used to be. She cannot register what might have happened to it.

From auntie's bedroom:)

AUNTIE: Hey! Hey!

(but the girl remains sitting there staring at the blank space. AUNTIE comes out, as usual ungroomed and looking dreadfully skeletal in her sleeveless holey nightie)

AUNTIE: Hey! No TV! Get that wax out, or you're going to get thick ears!

(She sees that the girl is not watching TV and stops from clipping her over the ears)

AUNTIE: Hee hee, I thought you'd snuck out to watch the idiot box. See how nicer the world is if you...
   (imitates a triumphant boxer)
take notice of the World Longest Champeen of India?

(She dances around the mesmerised girl in a parody of sparring, then returns to her bedroom chuckling.

SHANTI tries again with the remote control. She makes a sound that could be help or sheer confusion. It brings EKANAYAKE out of his room. He (sleepily too) crosses past the bed, the girl and the missing TV to go and sit on the settee, where he tries to read the paper again. He notices the envelope, picks it up, then puts it back where the thief had left it as not his business.

AUNTIE'S door opens again and:)

AUNTIE: Hey!, what've you done with my TV? What a little moll! By the Good Lord Who Lives Here With Me, I'll have your guts for garters.
   (then screech at EKANAYAKE)
She's knocked off a gal's only television! How rotten can you get!

(EKANAYAKE now also notices the set has gone and is likewise confused)

SHANTI: (coming to senses) Naan TV thiruda illai. I didn't steal anything.

AUNTIE: You're not getting thrown out on your ear til you bring it back!
   (to EKANAYAKE)
Call the cops!

EKANAYAKE: What cops, Auntie?

AUNTIE: Wake up or go back to sleep in Sri Lanka. That was the only friend I had in the world, that TV was! Handcuff her! Beat the living crap out of her!

EKANAYAKE: Auntie, she couldn't even lift it, no?

AUNTIE: Hey!, don't you get fooled too! All her muscle isn't just in her little toe.

> *(She creakily gets down on her knees to inspect under the bed, even though it is plain the TV could not fit under there. SHANTI gets down there with her. They scrutinise every square inch under there, before:)*

SHANTI: (whine) I was watching my movie.

AUNTIE: Bullsh!

SHANTI: I was too.

AUNTIE: Hey!, you think I've got feathers up me bum and can't fly?

EKANAYAKE: (to stop it) Auntie, what's this envelope?

AUNTIE: ('never mind that', still at the girl) You get next door and get that thieving mother of yours to give me back my TV! No mercy, no mercy!

SHANTI: Can't.

AUNTIE: Not half you can't.

SHANTI: ('so there') It's Sunday. She'll be watching TV.

AUNTIE: Hey!, never mind what she's watching. If them over there start getting mouthy you tell 'em from me I'll be over there and, pow!, smack in the chops, smack in the chops, come and get it!

EKANAYAKE: (trying to figure envelope) 'Mrs David'.

> *(AUNTIE swings over to pound on the door of the room where DOROTHY is)*

AUNTIE: Hey!, you!, letters!

> *(and angrily launches herself out into the kitchen.*
>
> *SHANTI throws down the remote control and follows her.*
>
> *At much the same time, DOROTHY emerges to have EKANAYAKE hold out the envelope for her)*

DOROTHY: (takes it, but:) God, my mouth feels like it's cleaned up Sydney's sewerage problem.

> *(She opens the envelope. There is nothing in it. She looks quizzically at him, and he points to where the TV used to be, as if by way of explanation)*

EKANAYAKE: The TV's gone.

DOROTHY: And?

EKANAYAKE: That envelope was left in its place, bloodypuckinghell sorry.

DOROTHY: I get an empty envelope for her TV? Bollywood movies still as bad as all that?

EKANAYAKE: Why 'Mrs David', not 'Mrs Sathianathan'? And if there's nothing inside, isn't it a message in itself?

DOROTHY: 'Itself' being?

EKANAYAKE: That someone's saying 'we know you are here'.

DOROTHY: This's too early for my jet lag.

AUNTIE: (returns shoving the girl towards front door) Go go go go!

(The girl starts to run but has no idea why, has to stop)

SHANTI: What?

AUNTIE: The thieving mongrels'll get away!

SHANTI: I want to go to the hole!

AUNTIE: Hey!, you go to the hole while you're chasing them.

(The girl dashes out, hitching up her dress)

EKANAYAKE: (scrutinising print on envelope) Where's 'Erskinville RSL'?

DOROTHY: In Sydney. Where else in the world would it keep its license?

EKANAYAKE: Dorothy, it can only a threat be and...

DOROTHY: (correcting him) 'Only be a threat'.

EKANAYAKE: It can only be a threat and linked to what happened to David, isn't it?, bloodypuckinghell.

AUNTIE: Hey!

EKANAYAKE: (automatically) Sorry, Auntie.

AUNTIE: Guts for garters, you, guts for garters!

DOROTHY: You're scaring me.

AUNTIE: Hey!, pardon piggy, but who's television is it? Mine, orright?, not David's. David didn't even own his own home.

DOROTHY: We did so, and you shouldn't go around saying that.

AUNTIE: ('so what?') Hey!, I used to own a television, that's all I know!

>(She stops when SHANTI returns. The girl casually strolls in; it certainly doesn't look like she been running much. To their raised eyebrows:)

SHANTI: (cheerily) I got to the hole.

AUNTIE: Where's my TV, you little squirt?

SHANTI: (surlily) Next door says they saw them.

>(EKANAYAKE hurries out.)

AUNTIE: (self pity) The whole thing stinks in my book.

>(She sits on the bed looking forlornly at where the TV should have been. The girl follows suit)

AUNTIE: (but very muted) Hey!, I put my nit pickers in a fire, you going to too?
   (*then, to no one*)
You don't know what it's like on cold nights and nothing to switch on.

DOROTHY: We'll get it back. We'll get a new one.

AUNTIE: Hey!, you still here? Come here and be useful.

>(She motions DOROTHY to sit next to her and to stare at the vacant TV space. Finally:)

DOROTHY: (whisper) What are we doing?

AUNTIE: We're asking the Lord to bring my box back.

DOROTHY: Oh.

AUNTIE: Hey!, He lives here too. Don't think He doesn't miss what some thieving magpie has taken.

> *(Long pause before EKANAYAKE returns. He motions to them to give him a moment, gets his mobile phone, then rings his seconded department at the Indian CBI)*

EKANAYAKE: Chief Inspector Ekanayake, Sri Lankan CID here. No, I am not ringing overseas up from, is it? No, I'm not Skype. Who's Skype?, bloodypuckinghell sorry Auntie. Put me through to the Duty Officer, please. What? I know there's no Duty Officer called Skype. I didn't ask for any Duty Office called Skype. Yes, yes, I won't go bitching if you put me through to whoever you've got.
  (*then*)
Bloodypuckinghell. Sorry, Auntie, sorry.
  (*back into phone*)
Ah, yes, Ekanayake here, Tharoor. Yes, the Sri Lankan long tall drink of water. Listen, Tharoor, from here, a three-wheeler described as red with a blacktop torn all over, covered registration number all up... yes, I know all tuk-tuks look like that. Two men, isn't it?, carrying a TV. What? Yes, my home here. What? Yes, they just walked in and walked right out, isn't it? Me? Yes, I was here at the time, wasn't it? Hey, what's funny?! Bloodypuckinghell!

AUNTIE: Hey!, I'll come over there and clock you one.

EKANAYAKE: Sorry, sorry, Auntie.
  (*hangs up in disgust*)
I'll give him that's-funny. Next door, they thought they were the TV repairmen.
  (*turns DOROTHY's attention to envelope again*)

Did David being Tamil mean anything normal than more to you?

DOROTHY: 'More than normal'. With a name like Sathiblahblahblah, I couldn't even spell let alone pronounce, I wasn't going to forget it, sure. But no, we never even talked about your mob or his mob or any of that Sri Lanka mob stuff. Back home, it doesn't gel. But if what you're implying is what I think you are... how come they could know I was here so quickly?

EKANAYAKE: About David, they hadn't arrested anyone in Sydney yet, isn't it?

DOROTHY: I told you I don't know. You'd know that quicker than me. Or your Interpol thing would.

EKANAYAKE: (a quiet command) Perhaps we should be talking about what really happened, no? Auntie...?

AUNTIE: (but heart not in it) Hey!, don't go dragging a gal into this.

> *(She gets up listlessly, moves into kitchen. DOROTHY doesn't want to say anything without her there:)*

DOROTHY: Sorry, Charlie. I know you think something's going on, but she's got the right to hear it first. I guess that means when she wants to.

EKANAYAKE: Aiyyo, I didn't mean anything like that.

DOROTHY: No, you're right. The moment I walked through this door I realised this was all hopeless. With David, it was all right...just... but she's so frail, you know. No, so *foreign*, like. She frightens me! And Navin, he's like a gun you want to put to your own head, you know?
 (*near panic*)
Do you know the sheer horror David must have gone through?

EKANAYAKE: I'll be frank, Dorothy. You could be in danger. If you are, then Auntie could be too.

DOROTHY: You're right. I'm sorry. But why us?

EKANAYAKE: (indicates phone) Tharoor will be knowing what he should be looking for.

(AUNTIE returns, at first not catching sight of SHANTI on the front doorstep doing nothing)

AUNTIE: Hey!, that little moll thinks I'm the lamp post and she's the dog!
  (sees her)
Well, Miss Ants-Up-Her-Pants, lift your leg on this: that dopey mother of yours is on her way and no mercy this time!

SHANTI: You didn't see her, you old woman.

AUNTIE: (sparring) Hey!, put 'em up, you!

EKANAYAKE: Don't talk to Auntie like that, girl.

AUNTIE: (placated) Did you get to that pump? I want that water on before you leave here.
  (the girl shuffles ill-humouredly back into the kitchen)
Hey!, I want to see black tea top of the menu here. Got that?
  (then to them)
How's a poor old lady who doesn't ask much gonna get her Sunday night movie tonight?

EKANAYAKE: Do you want me to go down the shop and buy one?

AUNTIE: (instant cunning again) Buy what?

EKANAYAKE: (wishing he hadn't spoken) A television.

(Both women stare at him, probably trying to gauge

whether he would actually do it. He shrugs, turns away from them. AUNTIE claps her hands)

AUNTIE: Open that man's pockets and get out the moth balls.
  (*leaves for kitchen*)
Hey!, what's going on in here?

  (Pause)

DOROTHY: On top of all this, I can't help thinking about that girl's condition.
I mean, she came just about when we were leaving. If she was up the oven before wouldn't she be showing more?

EKANAYAKE: I don't know, isn't it?

DOROTHY: Does she get any days off to go... kicking up her heels? And that's a terrible thought for a start.

EKANAYAKE: What are you saying, Dorothy?

DOROTHY: Well, I don't mean you obviously.

EKANAYAKE: You don't mean Navin?

  (They look at each other, then turn away with no little shame for having the nerve of even thinking it)

EKANAYAKE: (mumble) Karma, karma.

DOROTHY: (provoked again) Shit'n'sugar, you men should have it cut off at birth and have it left hanging on trees as a signal we women can know it's safe to twitch a muscle!

EKANAYAKE: (with warning) Dorothy, these people are obviously used to all this. Inferences. 'Mrs David' and nothing else. What are they getting at? Bloodypuckinghell.
  (*into air, automatically*)
Sorry, sorry, Auntie.

DOROTHY: I should leave, you mean?

(He nods the possibility)

DOROTHY: (another worry) I'm not really booked until the day after tomorrow.

EKANAYAKE: We'll fix that.

(He goes to use the phone again, but is rudely interrupted by a brick being thrown through the window in DOROTHY's bedroom.

EKANAYAKE runs off to see what has happened. DOROTHY stays rooted by the bed. The noise has made AUNTIE and the girl hurry in from the kitchen. The old lady goes to follow the Inspector but is stopped by:)

DOROTHY: Auntie, no!

(The urgency in her voice, stops AUNTIE in her tracks, but she continues to wave her arms and mouth to DOROTHY, 'What? What?...'

When EKANAYAKE returns we first hear him treading over broken glass and then see the iron rod he carries)

EKANAYAKE: (to DOROTHY) Right through the window and onto your bed, isn't it?

DOROTHY: Shit'n'sugar.

EKANAYAKE: They even know what room you're using. Quickly: first I tell you then something...

DOROTHY: (before she can stop herself) 'First I tell you something then...'

EKANAYAKE: ... I'm over here because the Tamil terrorists are not finished yet, isn't it? Drugs, extortion, blackmail. Guns. People smuggling. Anything they learned as the one of the worst terrorist groups in the world before that new one in Syria.
   (*then carefully:*)
Dorothy, is any of this ringing true when it comes to David?

DOROTHY: He wanted nothing to do with them and told them so.

EKANAYAKE: When?

DOROTHY: (but obdurately) A couple of years ago, when they tried to extort us. That was common in those days. Charles, I know what you're saying but I don't think I can help you.

EKANAYAKE: (sternly) You should not try to bring too much into this house, Dorothy.

>   *(He gathers up AUNTIE and leads her to her bed. She is still shaky from the shock)*

AUNTIE: (but feebly) Knock their blocks off, a kick in the cods...

EKANAYAKE: (calls) Shanti?

>   *(The girl goes in needing comfort too. When he has settled them both down, he returns to DOROTHY)*

DOROTHY: What now?

EKANAYAKE: We wait. They haven't delivered their main message yet.

DOROTHY: What do you mean?

EKANAYAKE: We'll just be keeping a good eye out, isn't it?

DOROTHY: It's broad daylight!

EKANAYAKE: That's why it must be them, Dorothy. Putting the wind up us, it's more raw in daytime, isn't it? But no hurry, no worry. One, maybe two of them at the most, no? Any more for a woman, they would lose face, no?

DOROTHY: That woman being me, right?

>   *(He proceeds -- rather cornily -- to stuff pillows under the coverlet of the bed, as though someone is sleeping there)*

DOROTHY: Oh sure, I see how that's going to fool the once worst criminal organization in the world.

EKANAYAKE: If I am not being too modest, there might not know I am staying here. They might be thinking I am only Navin. They must know when he's at home, he's always sleeping, so let them think that.
 (finishes with pillows)
Talk to 'Navin' as much as you can without feeling silly. When I go, do the needful and switch on the light, please. I will be locking the door behind me, so not to worry.

>   *(He slips out through the kitchen. She does what he wants with the lights, although not liking it.*
>
>   *A worrying silence. She goes to try to talk to 'Navin' but gives it up as just too ridiculous. She tries the settee and the paper. That's not much better)*

AUNTIE: (whisper off) Shanti?

SHANTI: (ditto) Auntie?

>   *(The old lady cannot answer for fear)*

DOROTHY: (needing communication too) How's the champion of all India in there?

AUNTIE: Blood oath I am!

SHANTI: (now laughing too) You, an old woman!

AUNTIE: (brave humour) Back of me hand, back of me hand, cheeky little moll! Hey!, Dorothy?

DOROTHY: Yes?

AUNTIE: Biff 'em all one!

DOROTHY: Too right! Biff 'em all one!

> (AUNTIE can come out now, but only in prayer mode... dirty towel on head and all. But her dynamic praying is not so dynamic. There is more than an element of self-mockery in it)

AUNTIE: God is Great! Hallelujah! Biff 'em all one! One right in the Righteous!

> (The girl mimics AUNTIE in forced high spirits. It is all so sillily defiant of the situation that it infects DOROTHY too. She jumps up from the sofa to join in... God is Great! Biff 'em all one!...' etc. Finally, they get tired.
>
> When they are finished, the scary situation comes back to them. Finally, DOROTHY grabs the phone, goes to dial, realises she's in a different country)

DOROTHY: What's the Emergency number?

> (they can't tell her. She tries to tackle the Chennai phone book, but it is a huge thing in Tamil, not English, and she has to give that up)

DOROTHY: How can you even lift this anywhere near your eyes?

AUNTIE: (*believing pillows to be Navin*) Don't bother asking little scaredy-cat Navin here. Not a bone in his willy, never had, never will.

DOROTHY: That's not Navin.

AUNTIE: (*prodding the pillows*) Hand off coccyx, on with socks, you little bugger!

DOROTHY: (needed release) THAT'S NOT NAVIN!

(*This shocks them all, including DOROTHY herself*)

DOROTHY: Look... Auntie...
   (*thinks about that*)
... all right, Auntie, why not? That's not Navin. Please... listen! I'm going to talk to you about David now, okay? Okay, you turn away from me as much as you like, but they shot him. They gunned him down. My David. Your David. In our own driveway. He was in the car. He was just going to work. They shot him through the right ear. I was running late. I was still locking up.

> (*AUNTIE puts one hand over one ear, the other on top of her head as though to hold down the praying head scarf. She sways with grief or perhaps a desire not to be listening. SHANTI quickly slides to the floor at her feet and lays her head in the old woman's lap*)

DOROTHY: I didn't come here to tell you what they must have told you. What I meant was...
   (*drives on*)
A twenty-two. No no; wait. A point. A point twenty-two, that's what they kept saying, as though that's supposed to make a difference. But... but it was David you see... right in front of me... and I had to...
   (*runs down*)

(It is then a frightening interruption when another rock comes crashing through the front window.

Outside there are shouts, followed by a sickening cry of pain and then ominous silence)

EKANAYAKE: (finally, off) It's all right, Auntie!

(He knocks at front door to be let in. Surprisingly, it is AUNTIE who has recovered enough to get there first)

AUNTIE: Hey!, who's going to get a clip over the ears?

EKANAYAKE: Sorry, Auntie.
 (then to DOROTHY)
Can I say 'It's all right?' or do I have to say 'It's all all right'?

DOROTHY: You scared us out of our wits and you want an English lesson?

(The old lady goes to look past him to outside where the moans are coming from)

EKANAYAKE: Don't look, Auntie.
 (dials on his mobile phone)
Detective Tharoor, emergency.
 (while waiting)
Auntie, have a lie down.

AUNTIE: (back to her old self) Blow that! What about me windows? What about me lawn?

EKANAYAKE: You haven't got a lawn, Auntie.

AUNTIE: (confusing herself) Who the shag cares? What's this little moll just sitting here for? What's a gal got to do to get some beauty sleep around here? Look at this pig's sty.

EKANAYAKE: (back to phone) Tharoor, Ekanayake. No, not from Bangladesh! From the desk next to you. Bloodypuckinghell!
(*automatically to AUNTIE*)
Sorry, sorry!
(*then takes it out on phone*)
Shut up, Tharoor! Bad man down here, get a bloody ambulance, isn't it? Okay, okay, I'll cover the medical costs if I'm lying, you silly bugger.

(*shuts phone off*

DOROTHY *meantime has braved inspecting the damage to the window. She cautiously goes over to look out the front door and is evidently fascinated by what she sees. He comes up behind her; just to her:*)

EKANAYAKE: You must do what I say if anything happens.
(*she nods meekly; he indicates 'out'*)
Surprised me by the rock through the window. She was quick. Well-trained.

DOROTHY: 'She' quick?

EKANAYAKE: She.

DOROTHY: Is she one of them?

EKANAYAKE: (nodding) She is the messenger I was talking about, no? Don't ask me what message yet. I'll see about that when she wakes up.

DOROTHY: Oh... 'wakes up'.

EKANAYAKE: (shrugs, then:) Tomorrow, we will have you on a plane. By the time you arrive home, Sydney will know what has happened here. You'll be all right there.

DOROTHY: (indicating outside) What's wrong with her?

EKANAYAKE: Apart from the broken leg? A bit of concussion.

DOROTHY: Shit'n'sugar.

AUNTIE: Hey!

EKANAYAKE: (demurely) It was their iron bar they threw on your bed. I just returned it, no?

> *(They are interrupted by a car. Then the gate opens and then the garage door opens)*

EKANAYAKE: Navin. He can do the needful, no?

DOROTHY: As Assistant Coroner, and gynaecologist? Depends whether she's dead or going to have a baby.

> *(She goes to look out of the door, but EKANAYAKE stops her again)*

EKANAYAKE: It might be for you not to go the door best... or the window... any windows... until we can get you on that plane, thank you.

DOROTHY: (surlily acquiescing) That's really terrible English.

EKANAYAKE: Sorry. I know it's the tongue's fault but they say they can't find anything wrong with it. Anyway, keep back just in case she has a back-up. Or...
　(confused)
her back is up?

DOROTHY: Right now you've got me spitting chips.

EKANAYAKE: (comforting effort) Even as we speak, Navin is looking at the patient.

DOROTHY: It's Navin. 'Looking' or really 'looking'?

(Finally NAVIN comes in.)

NAVIN: Charles, being an Inspector, there's a woman out there I think you should know about.

EKANAYAKE: I helped with the positioning.

NAVIN: Well, I gave him a thorough check-up, for which now I don't know whom to charge, if that wasn't bad enough. I mean what are the neighbours to think?

DOROTHY: Look, Navin, today ain't the day to come the snide remarks, alright?

NAVIN: But I wasn't being snide, dear lady.

DOROTHY: Blind Freddie could see it's a she, Navin, not a he.

NAVIN: (totally unapologetic) Have I come at a bad time?
   (*looking at mess on floor*)
Mother? The girl?

EKANAYAKE: (ignoring that as silly, indicating out) How was she?

NAVIN: Unconscious.
   (*at DOROTHY*)
That's why I couldn't tell he or a she, you know.

(She goes to say something, then doesn't bother)

EKANAYAKE: Broken leg all right, is it?

NAVIN: Oh, I didn't see that. Probably quite painful, I'd say. I always find someone being unconscious in the manner of not being subject to finger-poking, don't you know. Normally, with an iron bar like that out there, I'd say hmmm hit on the head. But I'll take the broken leg under advisement since you're the Inspector.

EKANAYAKE: Right, right, and how is she going to wake up, please?

NAVIN: Taking your word it's a woman, bit of the old smelling salts should do it.

EKANAYAKE: (over patiently) And do you have any? It would be helping the police work out a lot.

NAVIN (pleased at himself) Smelling salts in the car, quite possibly and absolutely

> *(But instead of going out to get them, he goes over to wash his hands at the 'table' sink.*
>
> *There is a loud and lingering moan from outside. [NOTE: For this first interruption, they are stopped in their tracks, but as the moaning goes on, they get to hardly notice it)*

NAVIN: I think I could give the Government a good saving on the smelling salts.

DOROTHY: (sourly) Maybe if we wait long enough we could go straight from the smelling salts to your dissecting table. We wouldn't want to keep the cockroaches waiting, right?

NAVIN: (not understanding) Dear lady?...

DOROTHY: (to EKANAYAKE) Charlie, what if there is another one out there?

EKANAYAKE: (not too worried) Since she's a woman, any other one's probably a trainer, watching how she goes in a crisis, etcetera etcetera. He's probably more interested in how to mark her for mettle.
  (*self joke*)
Not metal as in iron bar, ha ha.

DOROTHY: She's still dangerous?

EKANAYAKE: (shrugging) A few years ago I am betting she would be a suicide bomber. There is one other good thing, I think. A recruit... a woman who doesn't see me sneaking up on her... I am thinking this means the operation is not so high level as it would be if, say, you owed them money, Dorothy.

DOROTHY: Oh sure, me owing them money would be less important than killing me.

EKANAYAKE: Exactly. How could they get their money? For money, they are not sending any raw recruit, no? Anyone can cut a throat, but few are successful with getting the money back. This is India and Sri Lanka, nae?
   (*then*)
So you can see how I am so encouraged.

DOROTHY: (sarcastic) Oh, good. When I'm dead and gone, not a borrower was.

EKANAYAKE: (turns hard) They have to be connected to who killed David.
   (*then shrewdly at her*)
But poor David is gone. So what more are we thinking they are they after?

DOROTHY: (evasive) I'm not knowing.

EKANAYAKE: 'I don't know' is better.

> (*He pulls out a revolver, which he hands to her so forcibly that she has to take it.*)

EKANAYAKE: Miss Suicide Bomber out there had this. You must take it. It's not loaded now, is it?, but they are not knowing that. Remember, Auntie comes first if anything comes to... anything, please.

(He turns to NAVIN)

EKANAYAKE: Shall we?

(Reluctantly NAVIN nods. The two men go out to the moaning.

Without them there is a general lethargy there now. DOROTHY aimlessly sits, takes up NAVIN's advertising leaflet again, snorts derision again.*

She has just thrown it down with disgust when AUNTIE comes bustling in. She makes straight for DOROTHY, who half backs away, thrusts a pan and brush in her hand, then points at the shards of glass and so forth by the broken window:)

AUNTIE: Clean, clean.

(Then she simply wends her way back into the kitchen again. Behind her back, DOROTHY gives her a finger goose.

NAVIN and EKANAYAKE re-enter anyway)*

NAVIN: (chirpily, first to DOROTHY) You were right about her not being a man. And Charles here was right about it being a broken leg.
   (*evens-stevens*)
And I was right about unconscious.

(He doesn't have to tell them how the woman is, because the phone rings. He hurries as usual to get it first)

NAVIN: Yes, this is he. Oh, hello. Well, I would say the pain will either get too much or the patient will get used to it. Either way, the patient should quieten down before long.
   (*replaces receiver*)

That was the neighbours complaining about the noise. It's their Sunday day off. Christians, you see, but nice enough.

AUNTIE: (off) Hey!, who's paying for that phone?

NAVIN: They are suggesting we move the patient out onto the vacant lot on our other side. Not a bad idea, actually. Charles?

(EKANAYAKE does want to grace that with an answer. Anyway, AUNTIE comes in again, followed by SHANTI)

AUNTIE: That noise out there's putting the willies up next door's dog.

EKANAYAKE: It's nothing, Auntie...

(But she wants none of that. Shadowed by the girl, she goes over and throws open the front door. To another pitiable moan, she shrieks:)

AUNTIE: Hey!, we swept out there this morning!
   (then rounds on SHANTI)
What're you doing here? What're you doing with that water?

SHANTI: How do I know what you want with the water when I have to hit the hole?

AUNTIE: Hey!. I know what rotten reputation you and your condition's bringing to this Home of His Oneness! What am I, the chicken that laid the golden egg?

SHANTI: What golden egg?

(When there is another moan from outside, AUNTIE sits wearily on bed. The situation is actually badly affecting her)

DOROTHY: Charlie, can't you do something about her?

EKANAYAKE: (ear cocked) Not quite time yet, but soon, soon.

(AUNTIE gets herself to her feet, goes to the sideboard for some cotton wool, stuffs some in her ears, goes off to her bed for a nap. SHANTI shadows her.

EKANAYAKE himself yawns. With a depreciating shrug, he too goes off to his own room for a nap)

DOROTHY: (left with NAVIN) How can they hit the sacks with that racket going on?

NAVIN: India, Dorothy. It's outside. The sacks are inside, don't you know.
   (*indicates pillows under coverlet*)
Is this me? Passing likeness ha ha.

(NAVIN too lies down on the bed; she goes back to his leaflet, finds it even less palatable. She sits through the odd moan and AUNTIE's sudden snoring until she can stand it no longer)

DOROTHY: (waving leaflet) Navin, this is cock!

NAVIN: Please, dear lady. It's Sunday afternoon.

DOROTHY: Okay, for the sake of my David, I'll try conversation. I see here the 1000 rupees has been changed to 1500 rupees.

NAVIN: Regrettably, the 1000 was last week's. Inflation these days, don't you know. But we have increased our repeater's discount... the more pregnancies the less it costs. It's as far as we felt we could go... noting the 'we', you can see how I am not solely to blame.

(They are interrupted by SHANTI this time. She comes out of the room, again goes for the remote control and sits against the bed trying to switch the TV on. That it isn't

there, doesn't seem to bother her in the least)

DOROTHY: This kid's got tenacity, I'll give her that.

NAVIN: In all probability, she is sleepwalking again. Oh, and the marbles were a whizzo idea, thanks. No one the wiser. Except the crows, ha ha.

DOROTHY: (more concerned about the girl) Can't we do something for her?

> *(NAVIN misunderstands. He has another idea which spurs him to get up and go out to his car in the garage. He returns carrying his Ultrasound machine, puts it down where the TV should have been. He switches it on, then playfully replaces it probe in SHANTI's hand.*
>
> *He shows her how to run the probe over her belly to make moving images on the screen, which she continues to do mesmerically)*

DOROTHY: (heavy irony) That's real clever, Navin.

NAVIN: It is a fascinating machine, Dorothy.
  (*indicating its screen*)
See, there. And there. She's going to be fine.

DOROTHY: But that's not the point anyway, is it?

NAVIN: Beg yours?

DOROTHY: Is it going to live or die?

NAVIN: (again missing point, happily) It's doing your Australian crawl in there.

DOROTHY: (unamused) Is it a boy or a girl?

> *(He quickly ducks the question. Letting him off anyway she*

reads large painted letters he must have painted on the machine)

DOROTHY: And 'MBB' stands for what?

NAVIN: (Punch-proud) 'My Bread and Butter'. Ha ha. A little frivolity doesn't hurt, don't you think? I can be blamed there.

DOROTHY: My Bread and Butter. Navin, did anyone ever tell you what a knockout you are?

(The girl gets tired of watching the Utrasound screen, puts down probe, wanders out into the kitchen)

DOROTHY: Maybe that'll save her job. Get her to work in her sleep.

NAVIN: She's going next door. When she's half sleepwalking, she usually ends up there with her mother. She'll be all right.

DOROTHY: For a moment there, I thought something hot, wet and sweet might come out of that kitchen but I guess that's unlikely.
  (then)
Is your mother really giving the kid the boot today?

NAVIN: If she remembers to.

DOROTHY: Why? They're perfect for each other. They can drive each other crazy, and not spread the contagion.

NAVIN: What to do, dear lady?

DOROTHY: What to do?
  (then with loaded meaning)
For one thing find the father and give him to the nakkers.

NAVIN: What might nakkers mean?

DOROTHY: It means snip-snip then throw him to the shit house.

(and having gone so far, she openly stares at him)

NAVIN: ('no no') Dorothy, they tried to blame me a lot of accidents when I was an Intern, but I put a sign around my neck saying I could not be blamed for anything responsible. It worked quite well. I think it should be allowed to work here.

DOROTHY: And why's that?

NAVIN: Because my seed is home and hosed.

DOROTHY: Oh, home and hosed, is it?

NAVIN: Is it, dear lady.

(She believes him implicitly and gives up. Anyway, there is a most excruciating moan from outside. EKANAYAKE comes back out of the bedroom. He sits down opposite her)

EKANAYAKE: It's difficult to get in a nap around here, no? What happened to the smelling salts?

NAVIN: I will have to own up to only thinking I had some left.

DOROTHY: Hello?, there's someone in agony out there, and frankly I'm fast catching up with her.

EKANAYAKE: Right, right.
   (listens carefully to the pitch of another moan)
Soon, I am thinking. Please try to be patient.

DOROTHY: Someone half dead outside my door who's tried to do me in always makes me impatient. Silly me.
   (holds out the revolver)
Go and put a bullet through her head, then you can get a little nap.

EKANAYAKE: She's no problem, Dorothy. She failed. Even she knows her friends won't be wanting her to come back now. In fact, they will be keener that us for her to be shutting her mouth tightly. Why do you think we are waiting?

DOROTHY: I thought we were waiting for your lot.

EKANAYAKE: We are, isn't it? But when one thinks of it, she has no family to be speaking off anymore. Except us, when she gets around to a real good think about it. Having.

DOROTHY: You don't need to add the 'having'.

EKANAYAKE: Thank you.
 (*then at NAVIN*)
So, so?

NAVIN: So?

EKANAYAKE: (over another moan) So. Your little eye problem?

NAVIN: (delighted) Do you know with marbles all sizes fits all? A little sellotape and voila, thank you Dorothy!

> (*EKANAYAKE holds his hand up for silence when another moan comes, listens like a taster for a moment, then waves them on to talk*)

NAVIN: Dorothy and I were just talking about how a little technology fixes things quite nicely, don't you know.

> (*He taps the Utrasound machine in case EKANAYAKE doesn't get his reference*)

DOROTHY: (taking up the challenge) Look, Navin, sometimes I'm against abortions and sometimes I'm not. But...
 (*now her turn to bang the Ultrasound*)
this heap of shit... 'My Bed and Board'...

NAVIN: 'My Bread and Butter' actually.

DOROTHY: (bangs it even harder) 'My Bloody Butchery.

NAVIN: Please. The paintwork, dear lady.

DOROTHY: Paint the MBB over for WMD, weapon of mass destruction, you horrible... brother-in-law, you! You use this thing to see if there's something on or under the crutch, right? If it's under, you pull out the discount on oops there goes the umbilical. Right?

(She is so frustrated and angry she has to stop for breath)

NAVIN: Dear lady, I correct only if my patients insist on their patient's rights.

DOROTHY: Yeah, they decide which colour you big fat Mercedes will be!

NAVIN: Oh, unfair, Dorothy!

DOROTHY: Don't Dorothy me! Don't unDorothy me! I bet the only brown-paper take-away bag you've got sitting around has got a *dick* printed on it.

NAVIN: That's true. But then without our MBBs, where might our young modern Indian couple be? Think about going to all that waiting only to find you've opened your heart for one with no prospects of carrying all your hard work on, don't you know? It pains me to see you are blaming me all alone in any blameworthy stakes. After all we control the population crossing the streets, and someone has to get dirty painting the yellow zebra lines on the road.

(DOROTHY sullenly retreats to a corner.

AUNTIE comes out from her nap, moving groggily from a

cut-short sleep and unashamedly in her usual disgraceful attire.

There is, inevitably, another moan which, by now, only EKANAYAKE is really listening to, while:)

AUNTIE: Hey!, where's that little moll? Shanti? Shanti? She better not have left before I could kick her out. No mercy, no mercy. Who's up who for the rent around here anyway?
  (*to EKANAYAKE*)
Hey!, whatsyername, I'm not putting up with that racket outside.

EKANAYAKE: Sorry, Auntie.

   (He listens to another moan)

EKANAYAKE: It shouldn't be too long now. Auntie.

   (Now a bit lost by events, AUNTIE wanders off into the kitchen

   It leaves NAVIN all too ready to restart discussing his MBB pride-and-joy, much to DOROTHY's absolute fury)

NAVIN: Mind you, dear lady, I will privately admit we feel bound to offer no advice on our customer's decisions as to what weights on this hand and what weighs on the other hand. Given two fetuses of different gender where all things but one were equal we tend to give the nod slightly on the slightly heavier of the two, I might freely admit. If that little extra is because of a little extra jutting out, as it were, well, we find that many more go out the door happy to pay it. That's only good business, don't you know.

DOROTHY: HOLD IT RIGHT THERE!

   (He does so. There is a very awkward silence... even, it seems, from outside)

AUNTIE: (off) I'll come do the lot of you if you don't keep it down!

(At the next moan, the Inspector clicks his fingers 'that's it')

EKANAYAKE: Ah, I am being called.

(He is in no hurry whatsoever. Casually, he strolls into his bedroom, comes out again carrying a holstered gun, and walks outside.

Almost as soon as he does so, SHANTI comes running in from the kitchen -- giggling fit to wet her pants -- and escaping out the front door too. A long way back on her trail comes AUNTIE, hey-ing and puffing as she goes.

DOROTHY and NAVIN are watchers-on to this and to, a few moments later, SHANTI re-appearing in the kitchen doorway, while AUNTIE's angry face looks in through the broken front window. Next, AUNTIE appears in the kitchen doorway, then the girl gigglingly runs past her from behind to launch herself out through the front door again.

They carry on this even though they are surely passing by the drama with the injured woman going on outside.

EKANAYAKE returns. He is dusting off his hands)

EKANAYAKE: The patient can be moved, doctor.

NAVIN: (alarmed) By whom?

EKANAYAKE: We have an ambulance coming.

DOROTHY: The yellow submarine's safe!

NAVIN: (gratuitous explanation) It's not the blood in itself, it's more the plasma, don't you know. You boil it and concentrate it, and the villagers stick up broken pots and all sorts of things like mending roofs. Plasma plays the merry hell with new upholstery. It's in the manual; beware of spilling blood.

DOROTHY: And German car makers should know, right?

NAVIN: Exactly!

(The Inspector surprisingly rounds on her)

EKANAYAKE: So, Dorothy, how would you be knowing a man called Nanayanswarmy?

(She shakes her head, maybe too vigorously)

DOROTHY: (grumpily) Same to you with knobs on.

EKANAYAKE: What about Balalingam?
(*to her noncommittal*)
It is that just our new friend out there insists you know these people.

DOROTHY: 'It is just that…' And, like I've told you, if I can't pronounce then I don't know it.

(EKANAYAKE can see he should back off. But NAVIN is comfortable with any discomfort around him. He settles back on the bed as though leaning back in his clinic's chair)

NAVIN: Any further questions, dear lady?

DOROTHY: I hate it when you smirk, Navin.

NAVIN: (smirking) Yes, I've been blamed a lot for my smirk, I must admit.

(His further smirk only makes her more aggressive. She bangs the Ultrasound on the 'head')

DOROTHY: So, Doctor Death-Warmed-Up, how much would you say this cute little monster would set a hardworking gynaecologist back?

NAVIN: Oo, a pretty penny, dear lady.

DOROTHY: And what return would a hardworking gynaecologist get on one of these cute little monsters?

NAVIN: Oh, quite a goodly lot, actually.

DOROTHY: In round oops-little-she's-gone-missing terms, I mean.

NAVIN: Oh, in those terms?

DOROTHY: Yes, a pop.

NAVIN: A pop?

DOROTHY: (now furious) A POP! POP, POP! Out he pops; out she doesn't!

> *(There is an awkward silence around the extent of her reaction.*
>
> *Fortunately, this is interrupted again by AUNTIE showing real determination as she points the way out of the front door to SHANTI)*

AUNTIE: No mercy, no mercy!

SHANTI: (desperate) Not going!

AUNTIE: Hey! you get that fat-acre'd mother of yours here!

SHANTI: She's not my mother.

AUNTIE: Don't you lie in this house of the Lord My God.

SHANTI: (whine) My father will beat me, Auntie.
  (*brightening*)
Shall I go and come and show you the bruises?

AUNTIE: (stopping) Bullsh!

SHANTI: I could ask him for real ones like if I lived in Australia, Auntie.

> (*Surprisingly, AUNTIE stands her ground and points for the girl to go. It is a strong and uncompromising gesture which even the girl can recognise*)

AUNTIE: Hey!, what I said what I said. No mercy!

> (*SHANTI gets the message. Very slowly, very downcast, she backs out.*
>
> *It is a shocking moment for the others who didn't believe AUNTIE would really do it. For her part, the old woman sits back on the bed and stares straight ahead and her hands raised for no one to come near. There is nothing they can do anyway.*
>
> *It is almost a spur for DOROTHY to round on NAVIN again:)*

DOROTHY: Pop! POP!

NAVIN: (now sadly) Karma.

DOROTHY: *I hate that answer!* It ain't karma. It's POP. You squeeze and they POP. How much?

NAVIN: I cannot be blamed for the unique ways India choses to control its population, Dorothy. Not without prior written notice, I can't.

DOROTHY: No no, not as easy as that. Say, pops in a week. How many little shes you pop down the toilet a week?

NAVIN: (now on firmer ground) Actually, dear lady, all my patients insist on take-away, don't you know, so their husbands can see no cheating on a boy. Very sensible, really. We supply our own carrier bags, no charge.

DOROTHY: (really furious at that) Now, see, that was a mistake, you saying that. You are an awful human being, Navin!
   (*to EKANAYAKE*)
No, I'm not going to apologise. The whole damn world is banning these...
   (*bangs machine yet again*)

NAVIN: *Careful, please!*

DOROTHY: ... bloody things precisely because of that!

NAVIN: But that was just my little joke. They're not really printed paper bags. They're just ordinary paper bags.

DOROTHY: (rightly stunned by his answer) Forget it.

NAVIN: Not if it makes you so sad, Dorothy.

DOROTHY: I said forget it.

> (*But she regrets her backdown almost immediately and gives the Utrasound a resounding shove. NAVIN manages to save it.*)

NAVIN: (now on his own high horse) Machines might be inanimate, Dorothy, but they can go on strike, you know.

> (*He goes to walks out with it clutched protectively in his arms. But DOROTHY hasn't finished. She cuts off his exit.*)

DOROTHY: While we're at it… little Shanti, what if hers turns out a girl?

NAVIN: I already have the adoption papers ready him if she should wish that.

DOROTHY: I said she not he!

NAVIN: I know. You know, there are two types of people in the world, it seems. Some are happy about a fifty-fifty chance; others are unhappy about it.

DOROTHY: I didn't ask that!

NAVIN: Oh? I thought you did, dear lady.

DOROTHY: (getting it off her chest) What, say, if you're the father?

NAVIN: Never! And never say that!
 (*calms down a little*)
But I will say I hope to be his father and have already taken out adoption papers for him.

DOROTHY: But not if it's a girl.

NAVIN: (sad to say) Not if it is a girl, no.

> *(He now feels free enough to leave, but is stopped this time by EKANAYAKE)*

EKANAYAKE: I can't understand, my friend.

NAVIN: Charles, am I even going to get married?

EKANAYAKE: (meaning 'no') I don't know.

NAVIN: No. So, old friend, who's to send me on my way when my time comes if I have no son to light the pyre? Who can lift the smoke, but my own boy?

EKANAYAKE: (quietly) Yes, I see.

(NAVIN leaves)

DOROTHY: I didn't mean to insinuate… you know. Shit'n'sugar!

AUNTIE: (from bedroom) Hey!, hey!

EKANAYAKE: (calls for DOROTHY) Sorry. Auntie, why don't you have a little nap?

(DOROTHY decides now could be the time to finish off the relating she came to do. She stands by the bedroom door, doesn't go in, to speak to AUNTIE)

DOROTHY: Bite my head off, Auntie, but I have to get it over with now. Your David would have made you proud. He actually was quite famous. Thing is, you see, he deserved to be. They had just made him head surgeon at the Queen Elizabeth. I suppose the damn leftover Tamil-Tiger sadsacks thought he was enough of a big shot to set an example when he said no to their extortion attempts. I don't know. You'd best ask Charles that. But he was my...
   (again)
He was my husband. I liked being his wife. Did you like being his mother, you think?
   (then)
They shot him, Auntie. They shot him through the head in our own driveway.

(AUNTIE comes out of the bedroom slowly. She is placing the dirty towelling on her head, but doesn't have the energy to properly get up a dynamic chant. Instead, she sways listlessly in the doorway, only mouthing her chants.

There comes the distant sound of an ambulance)

EKANAYAKE: (could be talking to either woman) You'll be all right, won't you?

DOROTHY: You've still got to 'grill' me or whatever, don't you?

EKANAYAKE: (a yes) Auntie might be in danger too.

DOROTHY: Okay. Shoot.

EKANAYAKE: You are knowing this Narayanswarmy and this Balalingam, isn't it?

DOROTHY: Not the first. Balalingam is our next door neighbour. (*bitter laugh*)
Mansion-next-door more's the like. Dripping money. Our friend with the broken leg out there mentioned him, you said, but how come?

EKANAYAKE: The first man Narayanswarmy is her boss, a smalltime local crooked here

DOROTHY: 'Crook'.

EKANAYAKE:
He will be taken care of. But this Balalingam next door in Sydney, he was having a teenage daughter, isn't it?

DOROTHY: All bounce and new boobs. Early high school. Barely teenager.

(His implication comes home to her)

DOROTHY: No, you can't be serious!

EKANAYAKE: I am afraid we have to be, Dorothy. Apparently she was saying David was... eyeing her, getting too close. The trouble was... that one outside here says your David admitted it.

DOROTHY: Charlies, you saw David. He had bandy legs and his breath was really off. What good looker is going to...?

EKANAYAKE: It's a little bit more than that. A little while ago, she was off school for a long time? You stopped seeing her, isn't it?

DOROTHY: (nodding) I remember.
 (*stops*)
What's going on?

EKANAYAKE: Just a moment...

> (*The police arrives outside, as the ambulance earlier. EKANAYAKE has to go out and give instructions. These are brief gestures to get the woman out there packed off. He doesn't even bother to see it done, comes back inside*)

DOROTHY: (getting in first) She was pregnant too, right? And Balalingam thinks... knows or something?... it's David?

EKANAYAKE: We think he thinks you too, Dorothy.

DOROTHY: What have I got to do with it?

EKANAYAKE: The baby died. The girl tried to abort herself. Balalingam apparently thought someone had to be advising her.

DOROTHY: Oh, no.

EKANAYAKE: The girl had run away from home. In Sydney they should have told you all this.
 (*then*)
There's more.
 (*she waits*)

The girl tried suicide, Dorothy. She is... not right in the head anymore, and I'm told never will be again.

DOROTHY: (fatally) Balalingam had him shot, now the Tigers. Is that what you're saying?
   (*he shrugs but with no doubt*)
And that wasn't enough, right? He needs to kill me too, is that it?

EKANAYAKE: (nodding) Just a father. But not a building contractor for much longer.
   (*at a horn sounding*)
I must go. Will you be all right?

DOROTHY: What else can I do?

EKANAYAKE: (an asking for help) Will Auntie?

DOROTHY:(but 'yes') God knows.

> (*He leaves, and she follows to take a look*
>
> *They are no sooner gone, than SHANTI creeps in like a thief from the kitchen area. She leads AUNTIE to the bed and drops at the feet of of the old lady, holding on to one of her legs.*
>
> *Eventually, AUNTIE puts her hand on the top of the girl's head*)

AUNTIE: (no conviction, no energy) Go, go.

SHANTI: (but softly) No. You old lady.

AUNTIE: Go, go. No mercy...
   (*stops*)

> (*A long unifying pause, until:*)

SHANTI: (overplaying hand) God sent me back.

AUNTIE: Hey!, no blaspheming in this house!

SHANTI: He did too!

AUNTIE: (energy returning) I've lived with the Lord My God in this house for fifty-six years and He hasn't complained once. You think you can sit there and come between us, pull a woolly bull over your ears.

SHANTI: He's very sensitive to my needs.

AUNTIE: Hey!, Hey!, He'll smite your left little titty off, you talking rubbish like that.

SHANTI: (happily) No, He likes me. I might give Him a go.

AUNTIE: Hey!, I know what you are, you little harpy.

SHANTI: No you don't and I'm not telling any smelly old woman.

AUNTIE: What you'll get is a knuckle sandwich, you don't look out.

SHANTI: You, you silly old woman.

AUNTIE: Aw, dear Lord God, she's gonna be the death of me. Lord, dare I ask if the slack little moll's got that water on?

SHANTI: What water?

AUNTIE: That water! I told you the pump. Pump! You're making me spew.

SHANTI: It's my day off, old lady.

AUNTIE: That's it! You're outa here first thing!

(SHANTI gets up hurriedly, moves off into bedroom)

AUNTIE: Hey!, where're you going? Hey!, you use your own hole! Hey!

(But AUNTIE can't find the energy yet to get up to follow.)

DOROTHY returns. She too is badly at a loss. She sits on the bed next to AUNTIE. They surreptitiously slide nearer to each other. Finally:)

AUNTIE: Listen to her peeing in my pot.

DOROTHY: Thought I might see if I could stay on for a bit, Auntie.

AUNTIE: We'll have to squeeze you in. Hey!, no complaints, no complaints.

(They sit together while SHANTI finishes, comes out and sits with them. They keep watching the door)

AUNTIE: Look out, World; the world champeen of India's coming through!

(End)

www.ingramcontent.com/pod-product-compliance
Lightning Source LLC
LaVergne TN
LVHW051702080426
835511LV00017B/2689